SHAME

and the
Gospel

Transforming our view of the good news
and our Christian communities

Trevor Withers

malcolm down
PUBLISHING

First published 2022 by Malcolm Down Publishing Ltd.
www.malcolmdown.co.uk

24 23 22 21   7 6 5 4 3 2 1

British Library Cataloguing in Publication Data
A catalogue record for this book is available from the British Library.

ISBN 978-1-912863-89-1

Cover design by Esther Kotecha
Art direction by Sarah Grace

Printed in Poland

Endorsements

An accessible, very readable and urgently needed exploration of how to re-engage the contemporary, Western mindset with the good news of Jesus Christ, drawing on lots of fun illustrations from years of research and experimentation. A must-read for every Christian!

Andrea Campanale, Pioneer Network Developer at Church Mission Society and founder of Sacred Space Kingston

We have lots of books now about theology and shame. What is so brilliant about this one is that it answers the question of what can be done in practice about shame. Trevor speaks from years of practical experience in church groups, and it is so helpful.

Dr Rebecca Winfrey, trainee psychotherapist, theological researcher and author of The Cross and Shame (Grove Books)

Trevor Withers has given much of himself to explore the hidden epidemic of shame and how this relates to sharing the gospel message. Reading this book will give you renewed confidence to become more 'shame-aware' and therefore contributing to a more shame-resilient Christian community.

Sarah Grace, psychotherapist, publisher and author of Journey with Grace (Sarah Grace Publishing)

Make it clear, says Paul in Colossians about sharing faith. Making it clear means we must aim our message at the issues of today. Shame is carried by many millions deep in their souls, so let us understand it and speak to it. In this insightful book, Trevor helps us do just that.

Laurence Singlehurst, author of Sowing Reaping Keeping (IVP). Director of Cell UK and chair of Westminster Theological College

Foreword

I highly recommend both this book and the man who wrote it. Trevor Withers has been my friend for more than twenty years. Throughout this time, I have been a member of the church he has led – a church based on the principles you will read about in the following pages. These principles work.

We live in an age of anxiety. At ever-increasing speed, threatening storm clouds envelop us in their dramas. But our anxieties go much deeper. Increasingly we are lost. We no longer know who we are meant to be.

You may have wondered why the first reaction of Adam and Eve, after eating the fruit, was one of shame, and not of guilt. One of God's first responses was to make them clothes to wear. He was not just covering their physical nakedness. He was reminding them that he still loved them. Because when we cut ourselves off from the love and acceptance of God, we are indeed exposed. If people saw the real me, would they ever accept me, let alone love me?

The gospel is a many-faceted diamond. As Trevor explains so well, acceptance and love are key gospel messages for today. Today's felt needs are for love and acceptance – we crave someone to cover our nakedness and tell us how to live.

Ideas have legs, and love and acceptance are powerful ideas.

When we view the world through the lens of love and acceptance, a great deal changes. Love and acceptance are not just powerful evangelistic messages. They give us fresh eyes to see the kingdom of God in unexpected places and within unexpected people. They build bridges and reveal potential where previously we saw none. They make real the hospitality of the gospel. They dismantle the sides of our neat boxes. They turn potential battlefields into welcoming kitchen tables.

The principles in this book have shaped my work as well as my life.

They have encouraged me to go into the world rather than wait for it to come to me. They have taught me to value each person and their contribution. They have taught me to work within systems by starting from where they are. They have enabled me to make friends with many who might otherwise have been my enemies. They have taught me to earth my Christianity in this world, while still longing for a better one. They have helped me to build communities out of disparate voices. They have released me from seeking command and control and given me the courage to engage with servant-hearted leadership. As I say, the principles in this book work.

James Featherby

Chair of Medair

Formerly partner of Slaughter and May,

chair of CoE Ethical Investment Advisory Group, and

chair of Bible Society

Contents

Introduction

As a teenager, I loved taking things to bits to see how they worked. This might be my torch, parts on my bike or, on one occasion, I took my parents old radio apart, which fascinated me with all its electronic parts inside. I discovered that it was important to notice how things were put together and how the parts fitted with each other. If due attention was not paid to this as you took things to bits, it became very difficult to put them back together again so that they still worked properly. I was probably one of those children who was slightly annoying and always wanted to know why this or that had to happen. It just struck me as important to understand how things worked. This interest has extended into a desire to understand how our lives work.

My faith life has taken a similar route as a journey of exploration, where I have had conversations with God and others, asking questions, wanting to understand myself and hopefully in the process helping others grow and develop their own perspectives along the way. This has often meant taking some things to bits and re-orientating our view of God and each other in light of changing circumstances and new information. This is something all of us do, knowingly or otherwise. Life is in motion, it is not static, despite our best efforts to pin it down and minimise the disruption that life brings. I have lived through many changes in our culture as it has shifted from modernity to postmodernity, from Christendom to post-Christendom. These shifts have affected many areas of our lives and in particular our lives of faith.

One of the areas that I have noticed the effect of these changes is in how we share the faith we have with others.

In numerous conversations I have noticed a lack of confidence being shown by Christians about the gospel message and how we share this message with our friends. We feel that what we believe has little relevance for those around us.

So, I set out to ask some questions about why our faith didn't appear to be connecting well with our culture. I started to reflect on what was going on, to seek to understand, and in so doing, to take apart, as it were, the way the gospel message had been constructed, to understand it more fully and see if it could be put together in a way that made more sense in our current climate. What follows here are my attempts to do just that, in the hope that we will be able to effectively communicate both in word and deed the gospel of Jesus, and live faithfully as followers of him in the twenty-first century.

Many of us, particularly of a certain age, came to faith on a message of 'I feel guilty and need forgiveness'. Our evangelistic presentations and associated materials tended to communicate the gospel message with the need to experience forgiveness for wrongdoing as the dominant theme. This is also evident in much of our Church liturgy, which highlights the need for confession and forgiveness.

This pathway to God was based on an assumed moral compass that was a remnant of the UK's Christian heritage. Now the tide of this Christian heritage has gone out and we are left stranded on the beach, with no viable link to the new emerging culture. This loss of confidence for some Christians has undermined the belief in their own conversion. It certainly leaves them ill at ease as to how they can share the gospel with others in a meaningful way. I think this can feel like we are being asked to throw a bucket of cold water over someone which gets them wet and means we can then offer them a towel. What made sense for many of us once, does not any more.

Many of us have become aware that the way we think about the cross no longer connects readily with the things we see and experience in our Western world today. The guilt that we felt and responded to as we became Christians in our teens and early twenties no longer resonates in the twenty-first century. To share this shift and loss of certainty would make us feel like we are undermining our own conversion experience and invalidating our long-held tenets of faith. So we keep quiet. Not only in conversations with other believers but more importantly as we endeavour to put into words what it means for us to be a Christian with those who do not share our faith.

On the occasion that we do venture to offer a description of how we came to faith, or answer a question relating to Jesus and his death, we are confronted with bemusement or in some cases a sense of revilement. Now we can, of course, say that the gospel is offensive and challenging but also need to say that the gospel should be 'good news' that we share easily and with joy! Neither of these things seem to be the case, in my experience.

One of the changes that has taken place in our culture is the shift from guilt to shame: 'I have done something wrong' to 'there is something wrong with me'. Research by the author Brené Brown indicates that 'Shame is an epidemic in our [Western] culture'.[1] If this is the case then we need to rethink how we articulate the message of the gospel. We are not alone in this endeavour as Graham McFarlane, writing as senior lecturer in Systematic Theology at the London School of Theology says:

It is widely recognised that Western culture is undergoing significant change. What is less recognised by many Christians is the fact that, at each previous cultural shift, the church has sought to re-articulate what it believes about the death of Jesus. This is, after all, the *thinking* and *communicating* role of the church. It is *why* we have theology in the first place. It is not surprising,

---

1. Brené Brown, TED Talk, 'Listening to Shame', March 2012, https://www.ted.com/talks/brene_brown_listening_to_shame (accessed 1.12.20).

then, that there is renewed need to communicate the death of Jesus in vibrant ways for this new, *post*modern, culture. What worked for the past three hundred to a thousand years may not be adequate today.[2]

Therefore the aim of this book is to:

- highlight the challenge that faces us as our culture has changed;
- look at the changes that have taken place in our culture with particular reference to the shift from guilt to shame, i.e. 'I have done something wrong' to 'there is something wrong with me';
- look at how the life, death and resurrection of Jesus addresses shame, and what this means for the way we articulate and live out the gospel message in our culture;
- see how our Christian communities will need to be reformed as we work in this new world.

I think this is a timely issue and one that needs our attention.

My hope is that as you read you will:

- become aware of how our culture has changed;
- understand what this change means for the gospel message;
- gain fresh insights into the multifaceted nature of the gospel;
- be given practical tools to help you develop language and metaphors that connect;
- have renewed confidence in the message of the gospel to transform lives;
- have some understanding of the dynamics that will help to make shame-resilient Christian communities.

---

2. Alan Mann, *Atonement for a 'Sinless' Society* (Milton Keynes: Authentic Media, 2005). Graham McFarlane's introduction, p. xi.

I will reference a number of other writers, commentators and researchers, many of whom I have engaged with over the last twenty years or so. They have enhanced my thinking as I have attempted to live as a follower of Jesus. Closer to home, I have had the privilege of being part of, and helping to lead, a Christian community in St Albans and Harpenden called Network Church and I include many of the experiences that have informed and encouraged my faith from this context. I make no apology for referring to others as we are all finding our way together and can be encouraged and challenged through our interaction. We were not designed to 'go it alone', especially in these unprecedented times (we are in the midst of the coronavirus pandemic as I write). I am so grateful to be part of a supportive open and creative Christian community, which has acted as an incubator for so many ideas that have found their way onto these pages.

In particular, I want to thank a number of people: James and Charlotte Featherby for their encouragement and generous support which has enabled this book to come into being. Liz West for her help in organising my early ideas and putting them in some semblance of order. I am also grateful to Sue Pratt and Louise Chick for reading through my early drafts, and a special thank you to Louise who worked alongside me doing much of the detailed research.

Part 1
The First Signs of Shame

Chapter 1: The Challenge of Shame

It was a few years ago now that I first came across Brené Brown's TED talk on vulnerability[3] and shame. Something resonated with me, and if I am honest, I wasn't entirely sure what it was, but as her talk went viral, it became obvious that I wasn't the only one who had been moved by what she shared from her extensive research. Although I didn't realise it at the time, what I was sensing as I watched Brené Brown was a resonance within myself to the classic feelings of shame. The painful feelings of inadequacy and lack of value and loss of self-worth of somehow not being enough.

My interest in the loss of connection for the gospel with young people in particular and the possible role that shame had to play was also sparked by leading one of the regular reflection sessions with the team of Christians that work in local schools with an organisation called Step.[4] This is a team, supported by local churches, that goes into secondary schools to lead lessons and other activities, bringing a Christian dimension as they teach. We were looking at how teenagers, in the various classroom sessions and conversations over lunchtime clubs, thought about faith. We identified that a shift had happened where these youngsters were not feeling guilty about things in the way that we might have done at their age. They were, however, expressing that things 'were not right somehow'. There was a sense in which they felt ill at ease with themselves, not because of what they had or hadn't done, but rather about who they were.

A similar thing had happened some years earlier but from a different angle. I noticed that producing arguments that demonstrated that our

3. Brené Brown, TED Talk, 'Listening to Shame', March 2012, https://www.ted.com/talks/brene_brown_listening_to_shame (accessed 1.12.20); Brené Brown, TED Talk, 'The Power of Vulnerability', June 2010, https://www.ted.com/talks/brene_brown_the_power_of_vulnerability (accessed 21.2.22).
4. Based in St Albans and Harpenden.

faith was true only went so far in appealing to or convincing people that they should consider seriously what was being offered. This has always been the case, of course, because faith is a matter for the heart as well as the head. The Step director, Chris Birch-Evans, came up with a little phrase that summarised what we were observing: 'Young people are not so concerned as to whether something is true, they are more concerned to know if it works.'

This led to me coming up with the idea of what I called postmodern apologetics (apologetics is the defence of an idea through verbal or written arguments). This was a mixture of a more situational approach to apologetics, where the emphasis was more on the outcomes and consequences of any line of belief rather than substantiating its independent truth. This was a pragmatic response to one of the strands of postmodernity, which is a shift away from the overarching truth paradigm of objectivity towards subjective truths that are relevant for individuals, groups and communities of people.

Just after Billy Graham's death, I was at a church leaders' conference in Southampton. We took time to remember him and were reminded that Billy Graham landed on our shores for the first time in 1954 (I didn't literally remember, of course, as I wasn't born then!). He landed in Southampton on his way to start his London meetings on 1 March. We were told that he stopped at Central Methodist Hall in Southampton (the very building we were meeting in) on his way. He preached with great effect, seeing many people respond to his message. However, he used language that would not resonate today. As my good friend Laurence Singlehurst says:

> Words like 'sin', 'repent', 'saved' and 'born again' had resonance for them ... a great many of the hearers who came, whilst they may not have had an active church background, had nonetheless been to Sunday school ... Billy Graham also preached a gospel whose

connect-point was forgiveness: be forgiven; repent. This message, too, had resonance and power, the reason being that at the time, even though the government was secular, there was still a strong Christian moral framework in wider society… Conscience was alive and guilt was strong; therefore the message of forgiveness was welcome.[5]

At the conference, as part of our remembering this event, the twenties to thirties' age group were encouraged to come forward and stand on the stage so we could pray for them that they might carry the message of the gospel to their generation as Billy Graham had done to his. I could not help wondering what response this age group would give to a message using words like 'sin', 'repent', 'saved' and 'born again'.

One of the ways to look at this shift in culture from a biblical point of view is to consider the contrast between the Old and New Testaments. For example, we could ask at what point an important truth was conveyed in the Old Testament. The answer could be the receiving of the Law (the Ten Commandments) by Moses from God.[6] If we then follow this by asking at what point an important truth was conveyed in the New Testament, one of the answers could be when Jesus said: 'I am the way and the truth and the life'.[7] In this example, truth moves from truth on a tablet of stone in a legal format to being embodied in the person of Jesus.[8]

So in him we have our apologist, he carries and embodies truth, which becomes something that is lived out, that is practical and observable.

---

5. Laurence Singlehurst, *The Gospel Message Today* (Cambridge: Grove Books, 2013), p. 4.
6. Deuteronomy 5.
7. John 14:6.
8. Taught by Laurence Singlehurst in his teaching on *Sowing Reaping Keeping* training days, held by Cell UK Ministries, celluk.org.uk (accessed 8.10.21). See also Laurence Singlehurst, *Sowing Reaping Keeping* (Nottingham: IVP, 2006).

Shame and the Gospel

This moves truth from an objective fact that may or may not be relevant, to a living truth that is alive and dynamic and not recorded on stone but embodied in flesh and blood.

As the writer to the Hebrews says:

> In the past God spoke to our ancestors through the prophets at many times and in various ways, but in these last days he has spoken to us by his Son, whom he appointed heir of all things, and through whom also he made the universe. The Son is the radiance of God's glory and the exact representation of his being, sustaining all things by his powerful word.[9]

So we have glimpses of what God is like through the prophets, a bit like seeing the sun on a cloudy day. However, in Jesus we see God in all his radiance, as 'the exact representation of his being'.

Down through the centuries the Church has had to adapt the way it conveys the gospel to its surrounding culture; this is a process known as contextualisation, which in essence means making a connection between the context we find ourselves in and the message we want to share. It has been particularly true when Christian missionaries have headed overseas. In a new country and culture, they have to look for connection points for the words of the gospel message. I think we need to be engaged in a similar exercise, not by going abroad, but by simply recognising that our own culture has changed, so it may feel on occasion like we are now in a different country. This change means that the words we used to use to describe the gospel message and in particular, the death and resurrection of Jesus and what it means for us, no longer connect in the way that they once did.

In reading the New Testament, I have found Paul's letter to the Colossians such a treasure trove over the last few years as I have thought and reflected on the topic of shame. This is not because it deals with

---

9. Hebrews 1:1-3.

18

shame or even mentions it, but simply because it is so Jesus-focused and has so many helpful things to bring to us in our present times as we look at how we can share in a more relevant way the message of Jesus. These verses from chapter 4 have been particularly insightful:

> Devote yourselves to prayer, being watchful and thankful. And pray for us, too, that God may open a door for our message, so that we may proclaim the mystery of Christ, for which I am in chains. Pray that I may proclaim it clearly, as I should. Be wise in the way you act towards outsiders: make the most of every opportunity. Let your conversation be always full of grace, seasoned with salt, so that you may know how to answer everyone.[10]

Let's spend a few minutes with these verses from Paul's letter. I just want to highlight that what lies ahead of us here as we seek to rearticulate the message of Jesus, is nothing new. Paul asks for help in doing exactly this, as he says 'Pray that I may proclaim it clearly'. So, if Paul needed to think about it, and asks for prayer to be led by God and inspired by the Holy Spirit as he shared the message of Jesus, then we find ourselves in good company as we set out to do the same.

Here are a few pointers to take from this passage as we set out.

Let's start by looking at something which is simple and somewhat obvious, but can easily be over looked. 'Devote yourselves to prayer, being watchful and thankful.' Let us, then, set our minds to be prayerful as we explore together. Interesting that Paul uses the words 'watchful' and 'thankful'; I have been surprised how much I have had my eyes opened as I have thought and prayed about how we share the gospel. I have become watchful in two ways.

Firstly, observing my own reactions to the things I have discovered – if you like, a sort of internal watching; this should come as no surprise

---

10. Colossians 4:2-6.

to us, as it is a natural reaction to new ideas and concepts. Sometimes I have found myself wrestling internally, trying to get my head into a completely different space. Don't be deterred by this – if you find yourself reacting strongly to some of the concepts I propose, can I encourage you to wrestle as I have? Secondly, I have found myself noticing things in conversation; in particular, as I have run workshops on the topic, and have encountered other people's reactions. So be aware that shame and its effects turn up all over the place. I would encourage you, as you read, to be watchful of both your reactions to the text and its ideas, but also ask that God might reveal to you in fresh ways where our culture is showing signs of shame behaviour.

Some of your personal reactions may feel a bit disturbing, as many of us have had a particular view of what the gospel looks like and how we describe its message. This is the core of what we believe, and alternatives can appear to undermine the very heart of our faith. Let me be clear at the outset. I am not trying to say that what we believed and articulated before was in any way wrong. It was and still is appropriate. It simply is one particular way we can attempt to understand what Paul helpfully calls in the passage above 'the mystery of Christ'.

What I am proposing here is that we expand our horizons and look at other ideas that may be more helpful in our current situation. When I run workshops to look at shame and the gospel I often start by playing the theme tune from *The Big Country*.[11] This is a Western, starring Gregory Peck, and directed by William Wyler. The music by Jerome Moross is stunning and creates a sense of excitement and anticipation, conjuring up the vast landscape of open plains, which is the setting for the film. You may want to pause for a moment and search for the tune online and have a listen. Allow it to open the space in which you are reading and ask God to stir an excitement about discovering more of him in the pages that follow.

---

11. 1958. Distributed by United Artists.

Let's get back to the verses once more.

Paul links 'watchful' and 'thankful' together in verse 2, so let's remember to give thanks to God for all he reveals and encourages us to grapple with together. I use the word 'together' intentionally and suggest that it's not just an engagement between me as an author and you as a reader. Think about getting together with others to talk about this. Maybe read it with another person or use it in your small group, if you are part of one. It is interesting that Paul uses both the plural 'pray for *us*, too, that God may open a door for *our* message, so that *we* may proclaim the mystery of Christ'[12] as well as individual, 'Pray that I may proclaim it clearly, as I should.'

I love the phrase that Paul uses 'And pray for us, too, that God may open a door for our message'. It certainly feels to me as if a new door has swung open for our message. A door that leads into new territory for many of us. A door that takes us into an often secretive area of shame. A door nonetheless that has been opened for us. I am reminded as I write of Paul's vision of 'of a man of Macedonia standing and begging him, "Come over to Macedonia and help us."' We read on: 'After Paul had seen the vision, we got ready at once to leave for Macedonia, concluding that God had called us to preach the gospel to them.' in the same way, our culture is crying out just like that man, 'Come over ... and help us.'[13] My hope is that as you read you will hear the call.

Shame is a universal challenge and is particularly heightened in the West at this time; as we will see, it has become a major and debilitating challenge for so many of us.

So let's take Paul's words to heart as we see the door swinging open for the gospel.

In this chapter we have looked at:

---

12. Emphasis mine.
13. Acts 16:9-10.

- how my own journey began;
- contextualisation of the gospel;
- Jesus embodies truth;
- Paul's prayer.

As we move forward, I want to share a few more examples of where I have seen evidence of the shift from guilt to shame. Perhaps you have noticed similar experiences in your own life. See if any come up as you read on.

Chapter 2: Back to School

Shame often shows itself as a loss of value and identity. I started to notice this loss in another context through the work of Step in schools that I mentioned earlier. The school's work team have very creatively designed a lesson called 'Ultimate Questions' that I had helped to run on a number of occasions. This is designed in such a way that it asks a series of questions, each based on the answer to the previous question, and so it takes you down a pathway that helps to unravel your worldview. The lesson is fun, as it is run in the form of a game. As I hosted this lesson, I began to realise that the pathway that so often unravelled was frequently very similar from lesson to lesson.

Many young people came to the conclusion that because they didn't believe in God, they had opted for choices that ultimately drew them to a humanistic conclusion, basically believing that they were here by accident and had to make the best of it, with little or no hope of anything beyond this life. They arrived at this conclusion not in the stark way that I have just described, but by answering a series of linked questions with debates along the way that drew them to this end.

What was very powerful and revealing about the design of the lesson was that it ran itself, in that the students saw this pathway gradually open up before them. They reached their own conclusions by answering the questions, not knowing where this would take them. Here is an example of the questions, answers and pathways that often played out in a lesson; Sara and Helena from the Step team have written the following reflections on the lesson and its effects.

Ultimate Questions lesson

Is God real?

The first question we put to students is 'Is God real?'. Even if the majority of students know straight away how they will answer the question, they won't have thought about it in depth, for themselves, before. It's fairly common for them to have adopted their parents' 'yes' or 'no' answer, but they won't have challenged or explored their parents' perspective on it. Even the students who say God is real can't say why they believe this – in most lessons, we've spoken to a student who has answered 'I'm a Christian/Catholic/Muslim/ Jew so I have to believe in it'. Occasionally, they will acknowledge that they believe in some kind of spiritual presence, but not the same one that their parents talk about.

The great majority of students try hard not to offend anyone, and some have answered (or avoided!) the question by saying that they believe that everyone is free to believe what they choose. For these students, this belief seems more important than the question of whether God is or is not real. Sometimes we've challenged this by stating that either God is real, or he isn't – the fact doesn't depend on whether people believe in him or not. Students are much more comfortable with the idea of a God who is shrunk down to exist (or not) within our human opinion and imagination, so this challenge always baffles them.

A lot of them can't get away from the idea of God as a human creature with advanced powers, so they struggle with very practical questions of 'Who gave birth to God?', or 'How does he breathe in the sky?', or 'How can one man create everything?'. Even those who believe in God quite often struggle with the question of whether he created everything – they're often more comfortable with the idea that he found our universe as it is, and decided to put life on our planet. The idea of a God who created everything is simply too big. (Christian depictions of God as an old white guy on a cloud have a lot to answer for!)

Science vs God

Students find it much easier to accept 'science' than God, even if their understanding of science is as weak as their understanding of God. The Big Bang theory and evolution have come up in every Ultimate Questions lesson we've experienced so far and are probably the most common arguments used against the existence of God, but not one student has been able to accurately explain the basics of either. They see science as much more than simply the study of our world – it's often argued that our world was created 'by science'. For many, lack of proof or hard evidence of God is a big issue. They talk confidently about scientific evidence against God, but can't go into any detail.

Many assume that science and faith are incompatible, but it doesn't take much probing (or listing of scientists of faith!) to discover that they haven't interrogated this assumption in any depth. We find it fascinating how willing they are to trust science, which changes with every new discovery and which they don't understand, above any suggestion of a god.

The afterlife

In most classes, the majority of students will say that they believe in some form of afterlife. A few (particularly in older year groups) will acknowledge that this belief comes from fear – they don't want to accept that there might be nothing after death, even if they don't believe in a god. In general, they're much more open to accept things like ghosts and reincarnation than the idea of heaven. We wonder whether this is because they can imagine these things within the physical world we inhabit – they struggle with the idea of a mysterious other place that we can't see or locate.

Suffering

Suffering is a major stumbling block to students' belief or trust in a god. Students with a faith don't have an adequate response when challenged on this point. These students will often argue (rather glibly) that suffering comes from God, but as a form of test or to teach us something. But the others are always quick to raise the issue of babies who suffer, and the injustice inherent in much of the world's suffering, and the students of faith don't know how to respond. The idea of Satan or forces of evil at work in the world rarely comes up.

Purpose of life

Many students are very quick to say that there is no purpose to life or humanity and that it's an accident. Students with faith will say just as quickly that they do have a purpose because God made them, but they can't say what that purpose is. In most lessons we will hear a student say that 'everything happens for a reason' – but again, they can't explain that reason any further.

After some more thought, many conclude that as humans we have the ability to find our own purpose, but that it doesn't come from a higher being.

They find it easier to think about humanity's purpose if they are prompted to answer the question on behalf of their friends. If you ask them whether there is any point to their best friend's existence, they'll give a passionate 'yes' and begin to list reasons including their friendship, the fun and enjoyment they have in each other's company, their support, their impact on the wider community, their knowledge or special skills…

The default answer seems to be that nothing has purpose because ultimately, we die. Even those who believe in an afterlife and think that the purpose of this life is to gain access to the next one, can't fully explain what our purpose is other than survival for survival's sake. But again, we will sense that this is a stance that they've simply adopted without questioning, because it unravels quite fast with some gentle challenging. We don't think that any of them truly believes it, because if they did, why would they have bothered coming to the classroom, or doing anything at all? But we need to think more deeply about why 'I have no purpose' is the default answer, and where this comes from.[14]

As you can see, what typically happens in these lessons is the unveiling of the dominant worldview and set of beliefs that is held in the class. The point of the lesson is to show that these dominant views exist and to highlight what it means and what the implications are for every individual. As is often the case with people's worldviews, the ideas are gathered from different sources in a 'pick and mix'-type way and pieced together in an attempt to make a whole. This process is done subconsciously, without necessarily taking the time or thought to look at what these ideas mean and how they add together, or where they may ultimately lead.

In this chapter we have looked at:

- beliefs and worldview;
- loss of value and identity.

---

14. Helena Trent and Sara Martin, schools coordinators, Step schools' work team. Reflections from the 'Ultimate Questions' lessons. For info on Step, see https://www.stepschoolswork.org.uk (accessed 8.12.20).

I will pick up on some of the areas that come from this very creative 'Ultimate Questions' lesson in the next chapter. However, before we head there, take a few moments to reflect and ask yourself what might have been going on for these students in relation to the shame idea.

Chapter 3: Learning to See

Here is another illustration of how we can understand this cultural shift we are experiencing. I remember sitting waiting for a meeting and watching a carpenter and his apprentice working on a pair of doors, trying to understand why they were not shutting properly. The master carpenter explained to the apprentice that a way to see what was happening was to firstly, step back and see the whole picture rather than just focus on the issue presenting itself. Secondly, he suggested they needed to exaggerate the symptoms of the problem. They were both on their hands and knees at this point and the carpenter put his long spirit level along the base of the door so it stuck out beyond it, making it appear twice as wide as the original door. You could immediately see the problem as the far end of the level was considerably higher off the floor than the other end. So rather than just plane off the part that was rubbing and stopping the doors closing properly, they went to look at what had caused the movement that they had now detected.

My meeting had to start, so I didn't see what happened next, but did notice as I left an hour or so later that they were fitting a new hinge on the bottom end of the door. I thought this was a great illustration of problem solving, stepping back and exaggerating the situation so you could see it more clearly.

This is what happens in the 'Ultimate Questions' lesson that we looked at in the previous chapter. The students are physically standing looking at the questions that are on the floor in front of them. They are seeing the game play out before them as the answer to one question leads them to answer the next question and so on. This means they are stepping back from the situation and taking an overview of what they believe and why. For most of them, this will be the first opportunity they have had to peer into the treasure chest of accumulated beliefs and values, and try to make sense of them in their entirety. In our 'pick and mix culture', as it is sometimes called, it is not only students who collect these beliefs and values unnoticed, we all do it, and there is not a shortage of people who want to influence us in this respect. This process is yet another outcome of postmodernity.

What also comes out in the lesson is the overextension that I mentioned in the carpenter's situation working on the problem with the doors. The students begin to see where the things they believe about themselves and the world originated from, and where this will take them. Just as the carpenter's spirit level exaggerated the problem and revealed the cause of the issue so, as the questions are answered and the path is walked to its ultimate conclusion, the students get to see where their worldview ultimately leads them.

If they start the game by answering that they don't believe in God, then they tend to end up believing that life is a result of chance happenings and a fight for survival and so on. They are then left with something of a vacuum around who they are and why they are here. Where they find themselves is outside any overarching story that helps them make sense of life and give it meaning. This loss of identity is palpable and creates a very real atmosphere that can be felt in the room.

This lack of confidence about who they are, and the hope that they lack are at the core of how they feel about themselves. They are, at best, an accident, because they do not fit in to any larger story and are not made with good intentions by a loving God, and at worst, they are a mistake, and not even meant to be here in the first place! There are, of course, a multitude of other reasons as well for this loss of confidence in how they feel about themselves and their place in the world.

This example from the 'Ultimate Questions' lesson gives us a starting place to see why Brené Brown's findings are true, and that 'shame is an unspoken epidemic, the secret behind many forms of broken behaviour'.[15] The sense of hope that the Bible gives us, not just for the eternal future, but now in this present life, will need to become a vital part of our message to connect with where these younger people are starting from. We will also need to focus on the value God places on all of us to counteract the feelings of being an accident or a mistake.

What is interesting about the reflections from Sara and Helena, is that the Christians in the lesson find themselves in a similar position to their non-believing friends. Many of them, although they have faith, have not 'joined the dots', so to speak, and certainly don't have confidence in their purpose for being here. The loss in the sense of who you are, of your very personhood, runs deep. It causes all kinds of fallout. Our own need to be affirmed in our personhood is a fundamental issue. This loss of that sense of well-being can become a vital connection point for us as Christians as we look at connecting the message of the gospel with our culture. We as Christian communities will have things to say about who we are in God and where our identity comes from as members of his family. The cross has things to say about shame, in particular the resurrection and ascension. We will have to shift our focus from a view of sin that focuses on wrongdoing, articulated through 'I have done something wrong and need God to save me from my wrongdoing' (the guilt talk) towards one that looks at the fact that there is 'something wrong with me' (the shame talk).

Postmodernism has transformed our perception of knowledge and morality in the 20th century. Postmodernists look upon ideologies, truth claims, and narratives with scepticism and distrust. Postmodernism deconstructs 'laws' and 'rules' as dominating and oppressive cultural systems. When people view moral codes as culturally relative or politically motivated, then

15. Brené Brown, TED Talk, 'Listening to Shame', March 2012, https://www.ted.com/talks/brene_brown_listening_to_shame (accessed 1.12.20).

their conscience does not feel 'guilty' for transgressing moral codes. Moral relativity undermines notions of absolute guilt or moral standards.[16]

Unlike previous generations, this current one has not grown up in a Christian moral framework. They have not, by and large, attended Sunday school, nor will those who follow in their footsteps. The average CofE church has just three children attending, and the smallest 25 per cent have, on average, no children in Sunday school at all, according to the latest Statistics for Mission.

> This data, collected by parishes a year ago [2016], shows the overall decline in adult church attendance to be almost twice as pronounced among children. The average attendance by children, defined as being under 16, fell by 22 per cent between 2006 and 2016, compared with a 13 per cent fall among adults.
>
> In the smallest 25 per cent of churches, the average weekly attendance by children – at church services or Fresh Expressions on Sundays or weekdays – was zero. In the largest 25 per cent it rose to 11; and in the largest five per cent it was 35. The median is just three.[17]

This means that we cannot rely on our previous means of communication, assuming that there is an intrinsic Christian moral framework in place that enables the message of salvation in terms of guilt and forgiveness to be encountered and understood. This framework is completely blown out of the water. You may say, 'Well, that's OK, all we need to do is preach it', and quote to me the verses about God's word not returning to him

16. Jayson Georges, 'Five Reasons the West is Becoming More Shame Based', http://honorshame.com/5-reasons-west-becoming-shame-based (accessed 1.12.20).
17. Madeleine Davies, 'Too few children in too many pews', *The Church Times*, 19 October 2017, https://www.churchtimes.co.uk/articles/2017/20-october/news/uk/too-few-children-in-too-many-pews-a-warning (accessed 1.12.20).

'empty'.[18] But hang on, what did Jesus say makes good soil in the parable of the sower? Let's just take a look for a moment: 'But the seed falling on good soil refers to someone who hears the word and understands it. This is the one who produces a crop, yielding a hundred, sixty or thirty times what was sown.'[19] The good soil on this basis is made up of those who understand the message. Not just hearing it but having it explained in a way that connects and makes sense so they can understand it, that's what makes it good soil.

So, the message needs to be communicated in ways that it can be understood and acted on. Not just preached as if nothing has changed in the hope that somehow, magically, it will connect and be understood. This means we need to use relevant language, language that connects. 'To be culturally relevant, we must articulate Christian beliefs in a manner understandable to people within the society in which the church ministers.'[20] The question, then, is, what are we trying to connect to, now that the Christian moral framework has gone? What has replaced it? Where are the connections as far as the gospel message is concerned?

Of course, I am not the only one asking these questions; however, I am surprised at how few of us are giving it much thought. Not tackling it has led to a real decline in effective communication of the message of the cross and its relevance for our day, which none of us would dispute is in desperate need of salvation. This has led to a silence amongst many longstanding Christians, as we no longer know what to say or how to say it, in a way that makes any sort of sense to people. Steve Burnhope agrees that we need to move away from our now outdated concepts and look for new words and metaphors. He writes:

---

18. Isaiah 55:11.
19. Matthew 13:23.
20. Steve Burnhope, *Jesus Saves... But How? Telling the Story of Atonement in Today's World* (A Kingdom Praxis Solo) (North Hollywood, CA: Basileia Publishing: An Imprint of Harmon Press, 2012), Kindle edition, location 30-31.

Scripture describes Christ's atoning work in a 'kaleidoscope' of ways. Moreover, Christian creedal tradition has never mandated one single understanding, not least because different eras and cultures perceive the human situation differently. Insisting on the primacy or centrality of the one model of penal substitution, centred in law-court analogy, is a relatively recent idea emerging in Modernity. However, such insistence is not just biblically unwarranted, but a potential hindrance to Christian mission in cultures where crime and punishment is no longer seen in pre-Enlightenment terms. The article suggests that in the developed world, relational categories – the restoration of broken, estranged relationship with God – offer a more fruitful starting point for explaining Christ's work than legal transactional categories, which depend upon a worldview and criminal justice system that people no longer live in.[21]

On top of this, many of us, I think, are wondering how it could have made sense to us in the first place, as the culture we now live in is so different from the one in which many of us came to faith. So we have moved with the culture and been shaped by it. This movement means we have lost some of the power we once felt the message had for us initially. This has the effect of undermining our confidence twice over! Now, in all of this we must remember that the Holy Spirit is still at work, and it does not all depend on us, but we do have a part to play here, none the less. Each one of us are called to give account for the faith we have, we should 'Always be prepared to give an answer to everyone who asks you to give the reason for the hope that you have. But do this with gentleness and respect'.[22]

Our focus on forgiveness has been driven by the idea that we had done something wrong, and this was easily established, as I have said,

21. Ibid., Kindle location 17-20.
22. 1 Peter 3:15.

within the Christian moral framework of the past. We had a plumb line to measure against. Now however, as I just stated, this is no longer the case. However, this does not need to overly concern us because we can understand the gospel in a number of ways – the 'guilt and forgiveness' metaphor is just one dimension of the message. The richness of the gospel gives us many angles to look at it from and provide pathways of connection onto our current landscape.

In this chapter, we have looked at:

- hope and personhood;
- the Christian moral framework;
- a different starting point for our message.

In the next chapter, we will look further at some of these areas as we consider how the loss of a 'sacred canopy', as it is called, has affected us.

Chapter 4: The Sacred Canopy

To look at the change in our worldview in a little more detail, let's use some ideas from Peter Berger's book, *The Sacred Canopy*.[23]

Berger makes the case that a set off accepted ideas in a culture produce what he calls 'sacred canopies'. These canopies offer protection and bring stability and meaning. He looks at how this sacred canopy has been deconstructed by secularisation, echoing the ideas shared above about the loss of a Christian moral framework.

I used this as a teaching aid one Sunday morning at Network Church and found that the sacred canopy idea really resonated with those present. We have one of those large play parachutes that young children enjoy so much. We held it over our heads and gathered together underneath it. This I explained was like living under this 'sacred canopy'. We talked about what this felt like together. We then removed it and talked further about what we had lost and how this affected us.

Berger uses the term 'nomos' to describe a society's worldview and all the things that come together to make this up. This includes the knowledge of how things are in the society and includes all its values and ways of living these out. The society through its own process of socialisation tries to persuade individuals that this 'nomos' is indeed true. In so doing, an objective truth is created that is seen to be unchangeable. This objective truth is created through a long series of choices on the part of the individuals in the society. Summarising Berger's work, Ira Chernus writes:

A group of people who maintain a body of knowledge, along with the institutions they have created, is called a 'plausibility

---

23. Peter Berger, *The Sacred Canopy* (New York, NY: Anchor Books, 1990).

structure.' The nomos will seem plausible as long as it is supported by a strong plausibility structure.[24]

We see this very powerfully expressed through the structures and belief systems of Christendom, which has been our framework in the West for hundreds of years with all sorts of consequences. We can reflect on how this nomos of Christendom destroyed other plausibility structures, often in so-called missionary endeavours. As we have gone through the shift from modernity to postmodernity and from Christendom to post-Christendom, we have experienced the tensions between our inner and outer worlds; this always happens when change occurs.

As our inner and outer worlds are in tension, so we lose our sense of identity and it feels as if there is something wrong with us. The shift that we have gone through as we have lost the 'sacred canopy' and moved to a more secular society has caused a dissonance for us and we have lost our sense of personhood and well-being. There is an internal dis-ease as we try to make sense of the changing objective realities that have little, if any, overarching framework or construct that enables us to make sense of who we are in the world.

In Berger's terms, we must 'internalize' the supposedly objective realities that society imposes upon us. We must feel that our inner worth, our inner sense of 'rightness', depends on conforming to society's way of doing things.[25]

It is little wonder that our sense of 'inner worth' has been undone, as we have lost the 'sacred canopy' that held our world together and, with all of its many faults, helped us make sense of the world. So in this time of upheaval in our worldview, where are the connection points for the

24. Ira Chernus, 'Summary of Peter Berger, *The Sacred Canopy*', http://web.pdx.edu/~tothm/religion/Summary%20of%20Peter%20Berger,%20The%20Sacred%20Canopy.pdf (accessed 1.12.20).
25. Ibid.

gospel message? I have hinted towards this already as we have highlighted the loss of our 'inner worth', to use Berger's terminology. It should not be a surprise to us, then, that current researchers are highlighting similar discoveries.

Many people do not feel as if they have done something wrong, as right and wrong have lost their historical reference point. What does seem to resonate, however, is the idea that there is intrinsically 'something wrong with me'. A sense of unease around our personhood, feelings of inadequacy, and being an outsider. These feelings are on the increase in our Western culture.

Brown says from her research that shame thrives around three components. She does this by imagining we could study shame in a laboratory and paints the following picture.

> If you put shame in a Petri dish, it needs three things to grow exponentially: secrecy, silence and judgment. If you put the same amount [of shame] in a Petri dish and douse it with empathy, it can't survive.[26]

I found this fascinating when I first heard it several years ago and began to think what it might mean for us as Christians as we contextualise the gospel in our current situation. We can think of the gospel as an antidote, which is like a medicine given to us to cure or counteract the effects of a poison and deal with the unwanted effects or feelings.

If, as Brown's research suggests, when shame is doused with empathy it cannot survive, then one area we could look at as far as our gospel message connection point is concerned, is its empathetic nature.

Here is the good news: this is a very strong part of the gospel and, of course, finds its focus in the person of Jesus: 'who, being in very nature

---

26. Brené Brown, TED Talk, 'Listening to Shame', March 2012, https://www.ted.com/talks/brene_brown_listening_to_shame (accessed 1.12.20).

God, did not consider equality with God something to be used to his own advantage; rather, he made himself nothing by taking the very nature of a servant, being made in human likeness. And being found in appearance as a man, he humbled himself by becoming obedient to death – even death on a cross!'[27]

In doing this, Jesus empathises with us and douses our shame with his empathy. 'Even death on a cross' – suffering the punishment, pain and separation that we all experience as part of our human condition. We could say that in death he empathises with us in the most profound way as he takes on our mortality completely. This obedience in the guilt framework is interpreted as obedience to the Father, but in the shame context it could be seen as being obedient to the constraints of our humanity. In choosing to act in this way, he is stepping right into our space and identifying with us in the most empathetic way imaginable.

The ultimate answer to empathy is the incarnation

We can describe empathy as having an ability to understand or share the feelings of someone else. The writer to the Hebrews describes Jesus as one who is able to empathise with our weaknesses. 'For we do not have a high priest who is unable to empathize with our weaknesses, but we have one who has been tempted in every way, just as we are – yet he did not sin.[28]

Jesus, in coming and living among us, is able to understand and fully comprehend our situation.

In her book *Daring Greatly* Brené Brown describes empathy as being a reminder that we are not alone, judgement separates us and makes us feel inferior and exacerbates shame, whereas empathy shows connection

27. Philippians 2:6-8.
28. Hebrews 4:15, NIV (US).

and offers us a ladder so we can climb out of the hole that shame puts us in.[29]

So here is a very solid ladder (to use Brown's metaphor) in our gospel analogy. However, we still need to think about how we explain it and what it means for our gospel message. Even at this starting point, we have a very real challenge to overcome first; let me explain what I mean.

The 'Talking Jesus' research highlighted that '40% of people do not realise that Jesus was a real person who actually lived'.[30] This means that for 40 per cent, at least, Jesus' ability to empathise with us is irrelevant, as they believe he was a fictional character and not earthed in history, despite the overwhelming evidence to the contrary.

So, we have to start a bit further back with this group in the 40 per cent, for them we need to substantiate Jesus in his historical context before we can move to his empathy, helping to deal with our shame. It is good that The Alpha course deals with this head-on in the session 'Who is Jesus?' and puts together a good factual argument backed up by different sources for Jesus' existence as a historical figure.[31] HOPE, driven by the research, have also recently published a resource to further substantiate this fact called *Who Do You Say I Am?*[32] This has been published as a direct response to the research findings and is beautifully produced in full colour. It is designed as a giveaway book for Christians to make available to their friends.

So, establishing the historicity of Jesus and unpacking the many examples of how he shares our humanity, understands our challenges and walks alongside us through life is the beginning of a gospel response

29. Brené Brown, *Daring Greatly* (London: Penguin Life, 2015), p. 81.
30. 'Talking Jesus', research carried out by the Barna Group on behalf of the Church of England, Evangelical Alliance and HOPE, 2015, p. 5. Available as a PDF from https://talkingjesus.org/wp-content/uploads/2018/04/Talking-Jesus.pdf (accessed 14.12.21).
31. Nicky Gumbel. Alpha manual, (Alpha International Publishing, 2016), p. 13.
32. Catherine Butcher, *Who Do You Say I Am?* (Rugby: HOPE & CV, 2017).

and, as such, acts as an antidote to shame. The sorts of ways we could do this are through the passages and stories that show Jesus' humanity.

The historical Jesus is one component of this, but another is that of the resurrected Jesus who, of course, draws alongside us just as he did with those early followers on the road to Emmaus.[33] I think this is particularly powerful because it brings Jesus into our current time and view. It lifts him off the pages of the Bible and out of history and makes him accessible to us, or rather, us accessible to him. He becomes alive for us here and now as he did for those early followers who experienced him in his post-resurrection body. The other post-resurrection appearances do a similar thing but not quite in the same way as this story. I think this is partly because Jesus is initially hidden from them as they walk along, as he so often is from us, and this gives us a particular affinity with the story.

We can also connect with the fact that the bottom has fallen out of these two disciples' world as the person they loved and followed has died. This shocks them and they are thrown completely by it, despite Jesus trying to tell them, during his earthly ministry, in John 14 for instance, that it was going to happen. Along with his death goes their dreams and hopes for the future. This identifies with so much of what is alive and well in our culture where there is a loss of hope and future well-being. Jesus listens and talks with them as they walk, again a simple but very effective picture of one who empathises, who literally comes alongside them. This empathy, remember, is what Brown highlights as the antidote for shame. This, then, is a mile away from the all-powerful, judgemental, distant God that so many in our Western world have in mind.

---

33. Luke 24:13-35.

Graham Kendrick puts this story to music so well in his early song called 'Comforting Stranger'.[34]

What happens in these lyrics is the connection between a historical event, namely the two disciples walking to Emmaus, and Jesus coming and walking alongside us as his contemporary followers. The words in the song include the metaphor of a lamp approaching us as we travel along the road of life. As we experience this lamp illuminating our lives, we know that Jesus is indeed alive and walking with us.

This is the connection we need to make as we bring the gospel as an antidote to shame: that Jesus walks alongside us, that he empathises with us, shares our sorrows and pain, celebrates our joys.

In this chapter we have looked at:

- secrecy, silence and judgement;
- empathy as the antidote;
- Jesus walks alongside us.

It's all very well having a God who empathises with us, but what part does sin have to play now? In the next chapter, we will look at the question of sin and how it relates to what we've been discussing so far.

34. Graham Kendrick, 'Comforting Stranger', © MakeWay Music, 1974, https://www.grahamkendrick.co.uk/songs/graham-kendrick-songs/paid-on-the-nail/comforting-stranger-i-took-me-my-walking-shoes (accessed 1.12.20).

Chapter 5: But What About Sin?

Because of our historical Western focus on guilt and judgement, we think of sin in a particular way. As we have already highlighted, our definition of sin is predominantly understood in terms of 'wrongdoing'. So we tend to think of sin more as our wrong actions rather than an inherent feeling that there may be something wrong with us, namely in our feelings about our identity or relationships. Because of this rather narrow focus on the nature of sin, it is often difficult for us to take on alternative views. This is one of the areas I would suggest we have adopted a 'nomos', to use Berger's language, and have taken on a particular view of what sin is, normalised by our Christendom culture. Let me take a few minutes to explain what I mean.

I have led a number of workshops with local church leaders and Christian workers, during which it has been interesting to see how discussions have unfolded about shame and its need to be addressed. The idea gets off to a good start, the problem is easily described and concepts are seen and picked up fairly well. However, there is an unease that what is being proposed does not really do the full job. You may be feeling this yourself as you read this book.

We have such a strong idea that sin takes on a particular form that we struggle to see it in another way. The sort of response I get is, 'This is all very well looking at shame, but we still need to deal with sin.' Whilst you can argue that there is a difference between sin and shame, there is also a huge overlap. Let me try to explain what I mean by this as we look at how we can see shame as sin, or sin as shame, if you prefer.

Because shame is based on a sense of loss of value and sits in a relational context, it is these ideas that undergird its creation. So a lack of value ascribed to God is seen as sin, and this can be demonstrated through not giving him the praise he deserves. It could also be misusing his name,[35] so dishonouring him. On a more human plain, if we devalue others in our words or actions, either in thought or carried out towards them, knowing they are created and loved by God, then we shame them and we sin in doing so. We can think of this as a move from the vertical and our relationship with God to a more horizontal plain that encompasses our relationships with others. Jayson Georges puts it like this:

> Moreover, sin leaves the sinner in a state of shame (i.e., isolation and rejection) before God. And most sin involves shaming other people, in not valuing them as God intended. Sin shames God, shames oneself, and typically shames others. This is, more or less, what I mean by the phrase 'sin is shame.'[36]

He helpfully clarifies further by looking at rule-breaking:

> Sin is not simply breaking a rule or law, but breaking relationship. When Israel failed to keep Torah they broke covenant with Yahweh; they shamed him before the nations. The guilt of law-breaking dishonors God; that is why law-breaking is sin. In Romans 2:23, the main problem is dishonoring God. Law-breaking (or more precisely, 'covenant breaking') was a primary way Israel dishonored God. Some of the most frequently used images for sinful Israel in the Old Testament is that of a harlot and adulterer (i.e., shameful/shaming people), not criminal or convict (i.e., guilty people).[37]

In clarifying our particular view of sin in the West, Georges reminds us that 'sin is a biblical idea; so it's not exclusively a guilt-innocence idea. Western theology has a rather guilt-based definition of sin – transgressing

---

35. Exodus 20:7.
36. Jayson Georges, 'Yes, I do believe in sin', HonorShame, 13 May 2015, https://honorshame.com/sin-and-shame-relationship (accessed 1.12.20).
37. Ibid.

the law, breaking a rule, or missing the mark. Consequently, Christians struggle to imagine a definition apart from legal language'.[38]

I have found it fascinating to see these dynamics at play as I have discussed some of my ideas about shame and the gospel in a number of different contexts. The first place I tried to do this was in a small, informal discussion group, which I set up for the purpose of looking at why the gospel message was not connecting in the way it once had. We met every other Sunday evening to talk. It very quickly became clear that it was extremely difficult for some in the group to move away from deeply held convictions about how the gospel worked. This looked quite mechanistic and highly transactional for them. I saw the legal language that Georges' highlights play a dominant part in our discussions.

It became almost impossible to move beyond this understanding, and my thoughts and ideas at that point were not developed sufficiently to be able to helpfully describe the new landscape of how all this might work in terms of the shame idea. As a result, the group only met for about four sessions. All was not lost, however, as it was a very helpful learning curve for me and highlighted where I needed to do more thinking. It also alerted me to the strength of feelings associated with the Western view of sin and salvation. The root of the challenge here was the focus on sin and its eradication through Jesus' death on the cross. The ideas around 'penal substitution' (Jesus taking the punishment for our wrongdoing) are strongly established in our Western Christian culture.

A second place where I have had conversations has been in local church leaders' meetings. My experiences here are similar but different, for a number of reasons. There is a realisation that alternative ideas and metaphors are needed, and some experimentation has been tried by some in terms of changing the language used. So, in some situations where a public response to the gospel is being requested, it's made in

---

38. Ibid.

terms of a reference to us not feeling good enough, rather than having done something wrong. It was noted that on these occasions there was often a slightly better response. However, when I then followed this up with questions about why this was and what the message accompanying the response was, I discovered it defaulted back to the 'I have done something wrong' concept.

So, we had initial signs that the request for a response needed to change, but no follow-through in how the message that accompanied it needed to look different for the response to make sense. Spotting this, I then tried to suggest how the message might look different and got complimentary nods of approval, but the ensuing conversations always headed straight back to describing things in terms of having done something wrong and needing to feel guilty so that Jesus could forgive us!

In this chapter we have looked at:

- sin as shame;
- shame as sin;
- a different emphasis in our gospel message.

We need to look at how the gospel message might be constructed so that it connects with the ideas associated with shame rather than just guilt. I have touched on this already in talking about the incarnation and its place in bringing empathy to bear on our situation and so apply the antidote to shame. In the next chapter, I want to share a personal story that shows the shame I felt as a teenager and how this played out in my life through one particular incident.

Chapter 6: A Personal Story

A key fact for the gospel and shame is that shame is relationally based. That is to say, it has to do with loss of relationship, and the restoration of that relationship as the person is reconnected through being honoured by someone who has a higher standing in the community. I had a very powerful example of this as a teenager.

I was not very academically astute at school, so had no sense of well-being in academic lessons. I was also not very good at sport, so was often amongst the last few boys left on the touchline when teams were being picked. 'OK, I suppose we will have to have Withers' still reverberates around my head.

Being excluded or on the edge was something I was used to at school. However, I could 'make things'. I loved art, pottery and technical drawing, not to mention woodwork. One particular project came together particularly well for me; it was an angle poise lamp, yes, all made in wood, and wired up ready to run. Our woodwork teacher used my finished lamp as an example to the class, and I felt 10ft tall (about 3m in current terms!).

What happened next, though, I could not have imagined and still to this day, I am amazed actually did occur. The woodwork teacher asked me to go with him, along with my lamp, to see the metalwork teacher, so we left the woodwork class together and headed across to the metalwork department. When we arrived, my woodwork teacher introduced me to the metal work teacher in front of the class he was teaching, and said, 'This is Trevor. He is really good at woodwork and has made this lamp. He will be doing metalwork with you next term and should do well in your class.' Can you imagine what that meant for me? I had found a place to belong where I was valued and above all, honoured by someone with higher standing in the community, in my case the woodwork teacher.

However, as I discovered in later life, this honour was bestowed because of achievement rather than inherent value. This is a theme that Mark Stibbe talks about in a very honest account of his schooldays called *Home at Last*.

Stibbe picks up on the hidden nature of shame which makes it hard to detect and deal with:

> The fear of separation, whether this separation takes the form of rejection or abandonment, is what leads the child to shut down, not just at school but often in the contexts they inhabit afterwards as well. Shame leads to fear and fear leads to control. This first manifests itself as *self*-control. The boarder learns from early on that self-control is valuable. Mastering one's passions – that ancient Roman virtue of the 'manly man' – is what matters most in life. Vulnerability is the very opposite of what it means to be a woman or a man. 'Control yourself' is the lesson taught by schools, backed up cleverly by lessons from philosophy and literature, recreation and religion.
>
> The trouble with this is that vulnerability is the path to wholeness at every level of our lives. Admitting that you're wounded is not weakness – it is strength. It is not cowardice – it is courage. As I have said a thousand times 'if you don't get real, you don't get healed' … Sharing your story of shame is the pathway to finding freedom from the chains that bind you. As long as you repress your feelings, shame grows stronger by the day.[39]

Part of evangelism in this context has to be creating atmospheres where hidden areas of our lives can be talked about safely, without fear of judgement. This is unlikely to happen in a chance encounter and is far more likely to be possible in an accepting and loving friendship where trust has been established and vulnerability is part of the atmosphere.

---

39. Mark Stibbe, *Home at Last* (Milton Keynes: Malcolm Down Publishing, 2017), p. 99.

For this to be the case, our Christian communities need to learn how to function in this way and develop these environments. For many of us, this will be a major change in our church life. I say this because for many, being seen to be OK and having everything together is what is often portrayed as being a good Christian.

A few years ago, someone who I had got to know was thinking about coming to church. She was unsure if that would be OK. 'Why would you think it wouldn't be OK for you to come?' I asked. There was a pause and then this reply: 'Well, I am recently divorced.' I thought that would be a very real reason to seek out a supportive Christian community. However, this person was fearful of being judged, found wanting and rejected. Her perception of church was that it was judgemental.

Judgement is one of the three components that Brené Brown highlights that shame thrives on. We are told that judging is God's job not ours, mainly because he is the only one qualified to do it. However, it is very easy for us to step into his job and do it for him. What would our Christian communities look like if they were less judging? What might we need to do to make this the case? You will be pleased to know that the lady in question did join us, and has on several occasions been thankful to be part of a loving Christian family. Not perfect by any stretch of the imagination, but committed to exploring openness and vulnerability.

In this chapter we have looked at:

- loss and restoration of relationship;
- the hidden nature of shame;
- vulnerability and judgement.

Next, let's look at the links between shame, isolation and being lost, and how this helps our reframing of the gospel message.

Chapter 7: Where Do We Start?

We can start by noticing that we are 'lost', which is a good word in the shame context as it identifies immediately with isolation, being separated from others. In one sense you have to show people they are lost before you can tell them they need to be found. You don't get the map out until you realise you are lost. One of the reasons Brené Brown has become so popular is that she is able to put words around what so many are feeling. She gives meaning to our sense of somehow being lost. As I write, her TED Talk[40] has had more than 50 million views!

As people of faith we need to do the same, in recognising how we, and those around us, are lost. I would suggest this needs to be done as an exploration rather than in a telling mode; as conversations, with an accent on listening. It is interesting what Jesus does, he uses questions, plenty of them. Conrad Gempf highlights this:

> In the first gospel to have been written, the gospel of Mark, there are 67 episodes in which there is any sort of conversation at all. Even when you are careful to count double questions as one – 'who's face is that on the coin? Who's inscription is it printed with?' – we have 50 questions of Jesus in those 67 episodes. And the pattern seems to hold throughout the gospels.[41]

Are we to assume that Jesus didn't know the answer to the questions, or was there another point here? In asking the questions, Jesus is often getting his listeners to think and work out why they believe what they

---

40. Brené Brown, TED Talk, 'The Power of Vulnerability', June 2010, https://www.ted.com/talks/brene_brown_the_power_of_vulnerability (accessed 21.2.22).
41. Conrad Gempf, *Jesus Asked. What He Wanted to Know* (Grand Rapids, MI: Zondervan, 2003), p. 19.

believe. This is just the sort of process I am suggesting here: to think about the sort of questions that will help people discover that their worldview doesn't hold together in the way they might have thought. In this way, we have an opportunity for them to discover that they may be in need of a map.

Thinking about it, though, a map may be a bit of a put-off as it pushes back into the overarching territory of modernism, and as postmoderns push against such ideas, then maybe the language of a friend to help them find their way would be better. This also keeps the metaphor in the relational setting, which is the space that shame occupies in the first place.

One question I like to use in this respect goes like this: 'Is the world as it should be, and if not why not?' People seldom answer that the world is fine, because they know it's not. What follows is then a process of verbalising why they think it's not OK as it is. All sorts of areas come up as the conversation unfolds, and you have a real insight as to the issues that they believe are problematic. Often this is the first time for many that they have tried to verbalise why they think things are like they are, and how they have attempted to make sense of them. Understanding where people are is crucial if we are going to make any sort of meaningful connection.

This conversation helps to give us some clues as to what we need to be looking at as the components in our gospel message as far as this person is concerned. This once again highlights the relational context; it's about this individual and how they experience the world.

We are all lost, and finding ways to recognise this and help people discover it and put words around it is an essential part of our mission. Here is another way of looking at this sense of lostness that is alive and well in our culture, from someone else who has become well known over the last few years, Dr Jordan B. Peterson, professor of psychology at the University of Toronto:

Another problem has arisen, which was perhaps less common in our harsher past. It is easy to believe that people are arrogant, and egotistical, and always looking out for themselves. The cynicism that makes that opinion a universal truism is widespread and fashionable. But such an orientation to the world is not at all characteristic of many people. They have the opposite problem: they shoulder intolerable burdens of self-disgust, self-contempt, shame and self-consciousness. Thus, instead of narcissistically inflating their own importance, they don't value themselves at all, and they don't take care of themselves with attention and skill … They are excruciatingly aware of their own faults and inadequacies, both real and exaggerated, and ashamed and doubtful of their own value.[42]

Just like Brown, Jordan Peterson in *12 Rules for Life* puts into words how so many of us are feeling about ourselves, and not surprisingly his book is finding a ready audience as well. So many are feeling less than they could be, unsure of who they are, so aware of their inadequacies. Our challenge is to draw alongside, empathise, and both share and demonstrate a God who reaches out, understands and cares.

One of the helpful places to start in this respect is to see Jesus' death on the cross as a continuation of his life. By this, I mean that Jesus' death came about because of the way he lived. He opposed the earthly powers of his day and offered a different way to live, which was based on humility and not authoritarian structures. This power confrontation led to his death. We have tended to remove Jesus' death from the rest of his life and disassociated it from the life he lived. We have developed our theories of atonement as standalone ideas. As Angela Tilby puts it, they have become 'forensic' in nature. She highlights how our understanding of the Bible, our use of hymns and the dominant themes of Western

42. Jordan B. Peterson, *12 Rules For Life: An Antidote to Chaos* (London: Penguin, 2019), p. 59.

Christianity teach a morality that highlights difference between good and evil. We speak in terms of a God who is seen rewarding those who are faithful and who punishes the wicked. Sin is seen as a form of trespass, the breaking of the law and in that sense, God is the judge and we are found to be guilty. God declares his verdict and we are condemned.

Tilby looks at how the Church's liturgy has also run along these lines and has reinforced this 'forensic' concept of sin as trespass:

> In the Church of England we knelt to admit, 'we have erred and strayed from thy ways like lost sheep'. ... At Holy Communion we confessed our sins in words of anguished emotional intensity, 'the remembrance of them is grievous unto us, the burden of them is intolerable. Have mercy on us most merciful Father...'[43]

Tilby goes on to explain how we feel that we are always in need of forgiveness and that we could not take it for granted. The God we believed in is angry with us and we needed to constantly be reminded of Jesus' death so that forgiveness could be extended to us.

So, we can see how deeply these ideas have become ingrained in our Western Christian culture and how transactional they are in their construction, making them rational concepts with, as Tilby describes, a 'forensic' nature. Like me, she has seen an unease with these ideas as our culture has shifted.

> The forensic view of sin is not the only way sin is understood in Western Christendom, but it has been immensely influential. Yet in the last fifty years there has been a revolt against it. The traditional liturgical language has come to be felt by many to be too oppressive, too guilt-ridden, too grovelling. People have come to find it difficult to believe in a God who responds to our

---

43. Angela Tilby, *The Seven Deadly Sins: Their Origin in the Spiritual Teaching of Evagrius the Hermit* (London: SPCK, 2009)., p. 5.

sinfulness with wrath, even just wrath. The traditional language of sin simply feels unreal and overdramatic. People today do not feel that they are that wicked as individuals.[44]

Tilby goes on to highlight what this means:

> The consequence of this is that people who are really concerned about their spiritual growth tend to take their real concerns elsewhere and not bring them to church. Feelings, say of guilt, or worthlessness; problems, such as compulsive behaviour; disordered thoughts of limitless power of revenge tend to be endured in silence or shared, if at all, with a therapist or counsellor.[45]

These are some of the things that those who are feeling shame will be experiencing; this loss of value resulting in a sense of 'worthlessness' – this is often linked to 'compulsive behaviour' as an attempt to fill the void. The very places they should be finding help and acceptance, sadly, their local Christian community, is often seen by them as judgemental and condemning. So the very people who should be finding hope and healing from a church community are feeling pushed away because they fear they will be judged by us.

> We want to be heard by someone who will take us seriously but not condemn us, and the fear may be if we take such problems to a priest, or express our feelings to a group of fellow Christians, that we will either find that our concerns are made light of or that we are rebuked in some humiliating way.[46]

So we can see that there is a need for change in the way that we approach this whole area, and it is not just a tinkering around the edges; it feels as if a whole part of our Christian heritage needs to be reevaluated. To use

---

44. Ibid., p. 5.
45. Ibid., p. 7.
46. Ibid.

my earlier analogy, some things need taking to bits and putting together again, with a different emphasis – one where God's acceptance and love is more to the fore, where Jesus identifying with us in life and not just acting as a sacrifice in death for us is more fully seen and appreciated. Suffice to say at this point that we have some very real work to do here, so let's take courage and press on to better represent the God we believe in to a needy world.

In this chapter we have looked at:

- we're all lost;
- Jesus' death as a continuation of his life;
- the language of law, crime, sentence and judgement.

In the next chapter, we'll explore why Jesus' victory over evil on the cross is so important to the gospel message for our shame culture today.

Chapter 8: Jesus' Death and Resurrection as Victory Over Evil

It would, of course, be completely remiss of us to be looking at how the gospel message connects with shame without considering the place of the cross, by which I mean the death, resurrection and in this case, ascension of Jesus. A note of caution is needed here. I have found to my cost that alternative views on how we see and talk about the death and resurrection of Jesus can provoke a strong response in some quarters. We are sometimes very connected to a particular idea or concept, often in this case it's the idea of penal substitution or derivatives of this concept. Where this is the case alternatives are, for some, quite disturbing and disruptive. I am in no way wanting to discount this particular way of looking at the cross, but simply to offer some alternatives that can sit alongside it.

The way that Western theology has dealt with the atonement has tended to disconnect it from the rest of Jesus' life in terms of why it happened. We take it out of reality and put it in a legal framework. It becomes a transaction, which can seem like the balancing of an equation in algebra. In this sense, we lose or disconnect from the reality of Jesus' personhood, and he can become, if we are not careful, a rather sterile component in the equation. I have purposely exaggerated the language here to make the point. This to some degree works fine when used in the legal framework designed to deal with guilt that we have historically applied to our atonement thinking. However, this approach does not help us when we are considering the relational concepts of shame rather than the legal framework of guilt.

The separation of the physical from the spiritual in Western culture has meant that yet again we limit the connection between Jesus' physical activity and his ability to empathise with us in this respect, and what we see as his 'important spiritual activity', as we categorise it. In this way, the very real person of Jesus is divorced from the divine. They are often kept, as it were, in separate containers. It is no wonder, then, with this in mind that we find it difficult to make connection points with the death of Jesus, which we have put in a spiritual transactional box as it relates to our salvation from guilt, and our situation of shame that needs empathy as its antidote. So, we need to remake this connection.

To help us make this connection, let's take a moment to look at what is described as the 'Christus Victor' view of the cross. This theme focuses on Christ's triumph over death and the 'powers and authorities'.[47] The church leader and theologian Greg Boyd[48] describes how many contemporary Christians don't realise that the more legal-transaction understanding of the atonement that we touched on in the last chapter didn't become a widespread idea until the Protestant Reformation during the sixteenth century. The view held by the early Church was different to this; whilst they believed that Jesus died in our place, it was not seen as a legal transaction but rather as God's warfare with Satan. As early believers and followers of Jesus, they believed that the main thing Jesus came to accomplish was to destroy the devil and all his schemes against us. This resulted in us being liberated from the devil's oppression; this view of the atonement has been labelled 'Christus Victor' which is Latin for 'Christ is victorious'.

Boyd highlights[49] that the New Testament idea of salvation is not an abstract idea but firmly rooted in our world. It represents God's confrontation with both cosmic and human agents that are against him. He then explains what salvation would mean from this perspective

---

47. Ephesians 6:12.
48. https://reknew.org/2019/01/atonement-what-is-the-christus-victor-view/ (accessed 21.2.22).
49. Ibid.

and how it would differ from our more traditional Western view of the atonement.

With the loss of a more spiritually dynamic worldview in the West the 'warfare' going on between Satan and God is not a popular concept in the way that it is in other places or times. I look in more detail at this in Chapter 15 as it plays an important part in our understanding of what is going on and sets the stage for seeing Jesus' death and resurrection in a different light.

> The early Church Fathers of the first few centuries of Christianity described humanities problem as bondage to the devil. Those who are deeply affected by shame are unable to break free of its clutches, and will be able to recognise their bondage to its effects, particularly if it is causing addiction or mental illness. Even if they find it difficult to believe in a personal devil, they understand that their shame comes from a source outside themselves. This explanation could be closer to their personal experience of what is wrong in their life than an explanation that they are miserable sinners.[50]

Some of the key scriptures in this view are that Jesus came to drive out 'the prince of this world'[51] He comes to 'destroy the devil's work'.[52] His mandate is to 'break the power of him who holds the power of death – that is, the devil'[53] and to ultimately 'put all his enemies under his feet'.[54] We see that he came to overpower the 'strong man'[55] (Satan) who keeps the world in bondage. He comes to end the reign of the thief who comes to 'steal and kill and destroy'[56] the life God intended for us. In this view,

---

50. Rebecca Winfrey, *The Cross and Shame* (Cambridge: Grove Books, 2019), p. 18.
51 John 12:31.
52. I John 3:8.
53. Hebrews 2:14.
54 I Corinthians 15:25.
55. Mark 3:27.
56. John 10:10.

Jesus died on the cross to disarm 'the powers and authorities' and make a 'public spectacle of them' by 'triumphing over them by the cross'.[57]

> Christ has in principle freed the cosmos from its demonic oppression and thus freed all inhabitants of the cosmos who will simply submit to this new loving reign. The cosmos that had been 'groaning in labour pains' because it was subjected to 'the bondage of decay' has now been, and is yet being, set free (Rom. 8:19-22). And we who were the originally intended viceroys of the earth (Gen 1:26-28) have also been, and are yet being, released from bondage and re-established to our rightful position as co-rulers of the earth with Christ (2 Tim 2:12; Rev. 5:10).[58]

So this shifts the idea of our salvation from a personalised sense of wrongdoing that I as an individual am saved from the consequences of, to a much larger scope and stage. Notice the totality of the salvation that is outlined in the following description and how it grounds our salvation in the realities of our earthly lives; this is not just a future salvation to be claimed in eternity, but one that has very real implications for the here and now:

> The Christus Victor model can simply take this to mean that Christ did whatever it took to release us from slavery to the powers, and this he did by becoming incarnate, living an outrageously loving life in defiance of the powers, freeing people from the oppression of the devil through healings and exorcisms, teaching the way of self-sacrificial love, and most definitively by his sacrificial death and victorious resurrection.[59]

---

57. Colossians 2:15.
58. Gregory A. Boyd, 'The "Christus Victor" View of the Atonement', https://reknew.org/2018/11/the-christus-victor-view-of-the-atonement/ (accessed 1.12.20).
59. Ibid.

In his book *The Nonviolent Atonement*, J. Denny Weaver, like Boyd, takes Jesus' death and resurrection and plants it squarely in the real world, and in so doing takes it out of the theoretical transaction box. He helpfully refers to this as the 'Narrative Christus Victor' approach, whereby the death and resurrection of Jesus is not seen in abstract terms when it comes to understanding the atonement, but rather is planted firmly in the narrative of the biblical story. He sees Jesus bringing about the transformation of social order through living differently and taking on the powers of the earthly realm that have set things up contrary to the kingdom of God.

Weaver talking about how white theologians have interpreted the Bible comments:

> Wth a few notable exceptions, they have debated abstract issues such as the relationship of Jesus' humanity to his deity but have failed to describe relationships between Jesus, salvation, and concrete problems such as oppression or hunger.[60]

This way of looking at the death and resurrection of Jesus reconnects it with our earthly experience, and in doing so remakes the empathy connection that is vital as we think about shame, rather than the more transactional and abstract constructs that have been developed around guilt. So Jesus' resurrection is not only to win the cosmic battle in the heavenlies. The emphasis is also placed on the battle won here and now and the difference this makes to the way we live our lives in the present and the transformation this brings both to us and the world we live in.

So, as an example we may take the well-known verse 'for me, to live is Christ and to die is gain'. Let's look at the context, which is that Paul will not 'be ashamed', but will have sufficient courage to live the victorious life that the 'Christus Victor' idea offers, and step fully into what Jesus has achieved for us through his resurrection:

---

60. J. Denny Weaver, *The Nonviolent Atonement* (Grand Rapids, MI: Eerdmans Publishing, 2011; second edition), p. 133.

I eagerly expect and hope that I will in no way be ashamed, but will have sufficient courage so that now as always Christ will be exalted in my body, whether by life or by death. For to me, to live is Christ and to die is gain. If I am to go on living in the body, this will mean fruitful labour for me. Yet what shall I choose? I do not know![61]

As we will see later, it is this courage that helps us create shame resilience.

It has always puzzled me why we get so focused on Jesus' death rather than his resurrection. With hindsight, I see that it has been caused by our need for Jesus to die in our place to forgive our wrongdoing. For a number of years my Easter Sunday message was preached around the need for us to step out from under the shadow of the cross and into the light of the resurrection. To make this point I crafted myself in true 'Blue Peter-style' a homemade necklace which had a 2in flat stone on it, the type that are great for skimming across a stretch of flat water. It had a very simple string affair attached to make it into a necklace, which I wore on Easter Sunday as I spoke.

It got to a point where everyone knew what was coming each Easter after a couple of years doing this, and could almost deliver my message from memory! 'Success!' I thought. 'Become people of the stone' was my encouragement, and 'move away from this focus on the cross'. I probably could not have articulated why I thought this was important or what was pushing me in that direction, but as I reflect now I realise that it was probably the start of my thoughts around this whole area outworking themselves.

The resurrection appears to be the dominant theme in the early Church. Weaver quotes research by Rita Nakashima Brock and Rebecca Ann Parker, which traces the evolution in iconography of Jesus from images of a resurrected Jesus in the early centuries to images of a dead

---

61. Philippians 1:20-22.

Jesus, which do not appear in Europe until AD960-970. Brock notes that until the end of the tenth century, a period she christened the 'Anastasic Era' (from *anastasis* or resurrection), 'incarnation, transfiguration, miracles, and the resurrection of Jesus were the central focus of Christian faith and art. The predominant focus was on Jesus' victory over death'.

> The shift to a dead or crucified Christ in the Eucharist separated believers from the living Christ. Instead of being humanity's forerunner in a journey to paradise and towards divinity, 'Christ became a victim whose power lay in his suffering and judgement against sinful humanity'. Instead of abundant life, he now offered 'judgement to be feared'. Where salvation had previously meant the enjoyment of community life in paradise, it now meant 'escape from guilt and punishment'.[62]

I think we need to refocus on the resurrected Jesus; this will be very helpful in light of where we find ourselves as we move into a new era with different perspectives. Recapturing some of the early Church themes around Jesus' life and returning to the ideas formed in this Anastasic period will be really good for us, and also help as we can earth them in an early Church expression.

In the same way that we think in the guilt paradigm, that sin in the form of wrongdoing leads to judgement and death, so also with shame there is a link to death. We are designed to live in relationship both with God and others. Our exclusion from relationships, caused by shame, takes the life breath away from us and in so doing leads to death. The ultimate punishment is often solitary confinement, it feels like, and is death to us. We crave and indeed need company for a fulfilling and fruitful life. We become who we are and are sustained in our sense of personhood and identity through our relationships with others.

---

62. J. Denny Weaver, *The Nonviolent Atonement*, p. 112. Quoting Rita Nakashima Brock and Rebecca Parker, *Saving Paradise* (Boston, MA: Beacon Press, 2009) p. 238.

Shame and the isolation it causes excludes us from these relationships and in doing so damages our personhood and identity and causes death in us. So, if we think of this in the context of Genesis, Adam loses relationship with God as he decides that he can be the one who knows good from evil. In making this choice, he becomes the centre of his own universe rather than letting his relationship with God determine these things. God comes looking for Adam in the garden and he hides in shame: 'For as in Adam all die, so in Christ all will be made alive.'[63] The death experienced is that of loss of relationship, the relationship that is restored in and through Jesus.

We have become so used to thinking of Jesus dying in our place to take away our sin (guilt) that it is difficult sometimes for us to see what might be going on here through another lens. One way to do this, which is helpful as we think about shame, is suggested by David Brondos in his book *Paul on the Cross*.

When we see Paul using the phrase that Jesus died 'for us' or 'for our sins', rather than interpret it in terms of penal substitution as we tend to do automatically, we need to look at it in its more original meaning which is 'on our behalf' or 'for our sake'. This sets the context for Jesus' death in his overall mission to bring in the kingdom of God, to come and show us how to live differently. In this way, he was building the foundations of a new covenant, re-establishing our relationship with God and one another; both of these dimensions are crucial to his kingdom mandate. He continued this kingdom activity even when threatened with death. He gives up his 'life in faithfulness to that mission, he obtained what he had sought for others when God raised him from the dead' (Brondos). Stated briefly, Jesus died carrying out his mission 'for us'.[64]

---

63. 1 Corinthians 15:22.
64. Weaver, *The Nonviolent Atonement*, p. 66. Quoting David Brondos, *Paul on the Cross: Reconstructing the Apostle's Story of Redemption* (Minneapolis, MN: Fortress Press, 2006), p. 110.

In this way, Weaver is building a case for the death and resurrection of Jesus being directly linked to the way he lived and not with some ulterior motive or somehow separate spiritual agenda. Obviously we can interpret Jesus' death and resurrection in a number of different ways, but as far as a connection with shame is concerned, I think Weaver is pursuing a path which is helpful. It highlights that Jesus was about establishing his kingdom on earth, a kingdom that he wants us to be part of and included in. It was the establishing of this alternative kingdom and the opposition to earthly forces that this new kingdom posed that led him to the cross. His new kingdom wins this battle as he is resurrected and calls others, including us, to continue his quest to see this new kingdom come, with the same hope of resurrection themselves.

In this chapter we have looked at:

- the 'Christus Victor' idea;
- the need to reconnect the spiritual and the physical;
- Jesus' kingdom being established on earth.

In the next chapter, we will look at the importance of personhood and how this can be established through the way we see the Trinity.

Chapter 9: Exploring the Trinity

If the antidote to shame is empathy, then this necessitates a relationship through which the empathy is conveyed. There is much we can say and need to say about our belief in a God of love, but in practice the God we believe in as Christians is still seen as distant and judging by many. A God who is angry with us is a common perception. We need to rebuild for ourselves, and those who we are reaching out to, a different way of thinking about the God we believe in as Christians. Along with this, we also need to consider how we see ourselves and the rest of humanity. Moving in our thinking beyond us simply being merely objects of God's love to seeing ourselves, and others, in more relational categories is helpful in this respect.

John Zizioulas, the Eastern Orthodox Metropolitan bishop of Pergamon, has some helpful insights for us in this area. In his seminal book *Being as Communion*, he outlines his thoughts on both the nature of God as Trinity and how that translates in to our understanding of personhood.

> Theology and Church life involve a certain conception of the human being: personhood. This term, sanctified through its use in connection with the very being of God and of Christ, is rich in its implications.

> The Person is otherness in communion and communion in otherness. The Person is an identity that emerges through relationship (schesis, in the terminology of the Fathers); it is an 'I' that can exist only as long as it relates to a 'Thou' which affirms its existence and its otherness. If we isolate the 'I' from the 'Thou,' we lose not only its otherness but also its very being; it simply cannot

be without the other. This is what distinguishes the person from the individual.[65]

So we can be seen as individuals and often think of ourselves in this way, especially in the West, but as persons we can only understand this idea of personhood as it relates to our relationships in connection with others. Increasingly we live in a world where we feel threatened by others and often only accept them if they are like us and do not interfere with our individualised space and constructs.

Zizioulas highlights the need for us to look at the Trinity as our basis for understanding how we relate to each other, and in particular, understand the link between relationship and the other.

> There is no other model for the proper relation between communion and otherness either for the Church or for the human being than the Trinitarian God. If the Church wants to be faithful to her true self, she must try to mirror the communion and otherness that exists in the Triune God. The same is true of the human being as the 'image of God.'[66]

What can we learn about 'communion and otherness' from the Trinity? One thing is that otherness is the starting point of unity. God is not first One and then Three, but simultaneously One and Three.

This takes our thinking around the Trinity out of the more abstract box of Western theology where St Augustine and other Western theologians have used words like 'substance' to describe the oneness of God, and brings it into the relational world of personhood were otherness is absolute.

65. John Zizioulas, *Communion and Otherness* (Kerala: Orthodox Research Institute, 1993), http://www.orthodoxresearchinstitute.org/articles/liturgics/john_zizioulas_communion_otherness.html (accessed 1.12.20).
66. Ibid.

Otherness is not moral or psychological but ontological. We cannot tell what each Person is; only who He is. Each person in the Holy Trinity is different not by way of difference in qualities but by way of simple affirmation of being who He is. We see that otherness is inconceivable apart from a relationship. Father, Son and Holy Spirit are all names indicating relationship. No person can be different unless it is related. Communion does not threaten otherness; it generates it.[67]

These are such helpful insights from Zizioulas and provide fresh perspectives for us from an Eastern theological reference point, which is very different from our Western view. What this often means is that it takes a number of readings of his words for us to start to appreciate what we need to see, and then work out how it relates to us and challenges our existing views. Our temptation is to look for simple solutions and take shortcuts to get to an outcome. Because we are now having to work in more relational terms as we realise that shame is a relationally based concept, we will be dealing with a whole new set of parameters and complexities.

Our interconnectedness will need to take precedence over our focus on individualism, which we have highly valued in the West. I love this statement from Hyde as he reflects on Zizioulas: 'Without proper relation to the "other," a human is indeed an "individual" but cannot be a "person."'[68] This is very insightful as it gets to the heart of the shame challenge, which is an attack on our very personhood as it disconnects us from the 'other' and treats us solely as an individual.

---

67. Ibid.
68. Eric Hyde, 'The Individual and the Church: John Zizioulas and the Eastern Orthodox Perspective', 27 December 2011, https://ehyde.wordpress.com/2011/12/27/the-individual-and-the-church-john-zizioulas-and-the-eastern-orthodox- (accessed 1.12.20).

So, a major part of our salvation with this in mind has to do with the restoration of our true identity, which is profoundly linked to our understanding of personhood. This understanding of personhood, in my view, is derived from our Trinitarian theology. Here our personhood is directly linked to and finds its meaning in our relationship to God and others. This to me seems like a good place to base our thinking as we continue to explore the territory of shame.

For a number of years I have used an interesting exercise to explore how we think of and visualise the Trinity in our Western worldview. I divide the group I am working with into groups of three. I then ask one person in each group to pretend they are the Father, one the Son and one the Holy Spirt. Firstly, I ask them to talk together about what they understand about each of the persons of the Trinity. I encourage them to talk in first-person terms to help them get into role and address each other in those roles as they speak. This helps to take the idea of the Trinity out of the rational box that we tend to keep it in and bring it into a more relational reality.

The next step in this exploration is to get them on their feet and strike a group pose to create a three-dimensional model of how they see or understand the Trinity. They are often reluctant to do this and continue talking and not getting to their feet. This in itself shows how we are so rationally minded that we are often resistant to experiential learning. I have on occasion had to go and be quite strong with some groups to get them of their seats and out of their 'head space'.

What happens next is always interesting. There is still a reluctance to work this out in relational terms by physically modelling something using their bodies to actually represent the members of the Trinity and how they connect together. They often continue to talk, but are just standing rather than sitting! A final, often forcefully delivered, instruction to start their physical exploration then has to be given.

There is nothing quite like the physical expression of something conceptual to get you to engage with the reality of what you believe. So the physical models that are developed are often very telling. I will not be able to do them justice in describing them here; you will have to use your imagination to enhance my written descriptions – or better still, find a couple of friends and work them out together in physical reality so you can experience them fully, and talk about them as you do it.

The most regular expression of Trinity that I have observed has a component that is common with many others, in that it is static: three people in a static pose as if having their portrait taken in a professional portrait-style circa 1930. The expressions on their faces also often look similar – serious and austere to say the least.

Another common component in these models is that of structure based around hierarchy, by which I mean a Father figure that is overarching, usually portrayed by the tallest person in the three. This person (usually a man) has his arms in an encircling-type pose. Beneath him is then the person playing the Son, arms stretched out, sometimes on one knee representing him being on the cross and in submission to the dominant Father figure. The final person of the three is often lying on the floor, or sitting at Jesus' feet and representing the Holy Spirit. None of the three have any direct contact with each other or are looking at each other. They are depicted as very separate, static entities that have come together to pose for the picture to be taken.

What this demonstrates is that we often have a non-relational view of the Trinity, one that is formed around our individualistic ideas of personhood. The ideas that John Zizioulas works with from his more Eastern perspectives create a model of the Trinity that finds its basis and understanding of personhood in and through the relationships within the Godhead. They are Father, Son and Holy Spirit because of the relationships they have with each other. In thinking of the Trinity in more individualistic ways (as is so often modelled by the groups) we miss the fact that we are caught up into this relational identity as we are created in God's image.[69]

Shame isolates and excludes; we feel separated and unworthy of connection, so our salvation in this respect needs to be about reconnection. As this reconnection happens, there is a renewal of our sense of personhood, which is now understood and indeed experienced in the context of the restored relationships.

So, as part of our grappling with connecting the gospel with shame, we need to look at the basis for our understanding of relationships and what they have to say about personhood and identity, driven, I would suggest, by our understanding of the Trinity. We would do well here to pay more attention to our Eastern Orthodox brothers and sisters, for whom this is far more familiar territory.[70]

From this relational perspective, our salvation is outworked in our experience of Christian community. At the risk of sounding controversial, we are 'saved' into and through our experience of Christian community. Let's look at Jesus disciples and how this worked in practice for them. The disciples had been excluded from their ongoing religious training as good Jewish lads. 'If they're fishermen and Jesus calls them to be his disciples, then they're not following another rabbi; and if they're not following another rabbi they're not the best of the best. They didn't make the cut.'[71] Jesus invites them to join him. They are not the 'best of the best' and in Jesus' eyes they don't have to be; they discover who they truly are as they become part of the community that he forms. They are honoured by his invitation and leap at the opportunity to leave their nets and follow him.

---

69. Genesis 1:26.
70. To explore further, see John Zizioulas, *Being as Communion* (London: Darton, Longman & Todd, 1985).
71. Rob Bell, *Dust*, Nooma DVD (Grand Rapids, MI: Flannel, 2005), https://www.youtube.com/watch?v=kM3qHBAekhg (accessed 1.12.20).

In the same way as we invite people to join our Christian communities, they will experience the God who lives amongst us by his Spirit and so get caught up in this Trinitarian relational flow and movement that we are invited into. As a friend of mine, David Viljoen, says, 'We are in some ways an extension of the Trinity as we emulate the relationships in the Godhead both in and through our Christian community life together'. So, salvation in one sense happens as we get caught up in the relationship of the Trinity, experienced through being part of the body of Christ here and now as we are born into a new family. Indeed, our very baptism signifies this; the early Church celebrated it as a door of entry into this new community. 'For we were all baptised by one Spirit so as to form one body – whether Jews or Gentiles, slave or free – and we were all given the one Spirit to drink.'[72]

In conclusion to Part 1: A summary

In this section we have looked at

- the epidemic of shame in our Western postmodern culture;
- how it links to a worldview which creates loss of value, identity and personhood;
- sin and shame are interlocking;
- the decline of the Christian moral framework in today's Western society;
- shame thrives on secrecy, silence and judgement;
- shame and its antidote, empathy, are relational not transactional;
- the need for a fresh contextualisation of the gospel;
- this contextualisation includes a new look at the Trinity, and at Jesus: his humanity, his death, his resurrection, his ascension and his victory over evil.

---

72. 1 Corinthians 12:13.

My hope is that our view of the gospel has been enlarged through these pages, and we have started to see some of the relevance of adopting new ideas and metaphors. These ideas, whilst they may be new to us, are not new to the Bible, as we have seen. As we move on, I want to look at some of the components that may help us as we think about how we connect some of these ideas in a missional space. This could be in a number of different contexts. Ultimately, we are all called to be witnesses. Jesus last words on earth as recorded by Luke are 'you will receive power when the Holy Spirit comes on you; and you will be my witnesses ...'[73]

My hope with this in mind is that we will all have some understanding of how we can share the gospel in a relevant way with our contemporaries. In our individualistic culture, the connection is likely to be via the individual in one-to-one conversation, although the ultimate aim is to offer an invite into a Christian community.

---

73. Acts 1:8.

Part 2
Towards a Gospel Message for our Shame-based Culture

Introduction to Part 2:

Towards a Gospel Message
for our Shame-based Culture

In this second section, my aim is to look at some key connection points for us as we share the gospel in a way that makes sense for our increasingly shame-based culture. The more we become aware of the way shame is at work in both our own lives and those around us, the greater clarity we will have about how we can connect the life-giving words of Jesus to both ourselves as we need saving from our shame, and those around us who have yet to discover God.

I want to do this in two ways. Firstly I will look at the context that we will need to create to be able to share effectively. We will then move on to look at a series of headline titles that will act as tags for us to use to develop our thinking around some key areas that I think will help us communicate well. You could think of these as Post-it notes reminding us of things we need to be mindful of.

It is worth remembering that shame is knitted into our culture, and carried by every one of us. It pushes us away from each other, separating us and making us feel isolated, misunderstood, and highlights our feelings of inadequacy. It permeates every area of our lives, our work, the way we parent, the very way we look at ourselves and others. We need to learn how to recognise its effects to find ways to talk about it and, through the transforming work of God in our lives, find restoration and peace with God, ourselves and others.

The words of Jesus come to mind here: 'The thief comes only to steal and kill and destroy; I have come that they may have life, and have it to the full.'[74]

---

74. John 10:10.

I think our culture has shifted and has become more shame-driven than guilt-orientated. A recent conversation highlighted this to me. It was with a chap in his twenties who said: 'We have enough faith in our own moral compass not to need to feel guilty.' We went on to talk about the more prevalent need in his age group around issues of identity, and shame.

With this in mind I offer the following thoughts and ideas as we are challenged to move in our thinking from a guilt-orientated worldview and how we explain our faith in that context to the emerging shame worldview in our culture and how this impacts our faith sharing.

Chapter 10: Secrecy, Silence and Judgement

Brené Brown's research highlights that

> If we're going to find our way back to each other, we have to understand and know empathy, because empathy's the antidote to shame. If you put shame in a Petri dish, it needs three things to grow exponentially: secrecy, silence and judgment. If you put the same amount [of shame] in a Petri dish and douse it with empathy, it can't survive.[75]

Our first challenge is to create a relational context that breaks the ties of secrecy, silence and judgement, and starts to create trust, vulnerability and acceptance.

Our starting point, then, is not so much in looking at the message itself but more at the messengers and the context that needs to be created for the necessary conversations to be held.

Because shame is about who we are and not what we have done, the relationships are key. We all shape the way we think about ourselves in the context of how others respond to us. Their responses to us and our reactions to them build a picture in our minds and emotions of how we see ourselves. I agree with the old aphorism which says 'we are not who *we* think we are, we are not who *others* think we are, we are who *we* think *others* think we are'. We are sensitised to the feedback that those around us give us; our personhood is formed by these relationships. This should come as no surprise as we are created in the likeness of God to be relational beings in his likeness[76] and are shaped by all our relationships, good and not so good.

---

75. Brené Brown, TED Talk, 'Listening to Shame', March 2012, https://www.ted.com/talks/brene_brown_listening_to_shame (accessed 1.12.20).
76. Genesis 1:26.

Our individualistic culture has, to some degree, denied this. We have been fed the message of individualism in our consumer culture. We can, it is said, 'Become who we want to be!' This is in isolation to the relationships we have around us and how they might influence us and the way we think about ourselves. In fact, it is often posed as a way to get away from the influence of others in our lives. Although this line of argument is attractive, it is fundamentally not true. Songwriters often use these relational dynamics as they strike such a chord with our reality, lamenting the loss and pain caused where relationships have gone wrong, often reasserting the need for independence and a cry for survival on our own, building walls around us to protect us from future harm: rocks and islands come to mind.

We find ourselves putting on armour to protect ourselves from the potential damage that can occur from the encounters we have with others. To create atmospheres where this armour can start to be removed is perhaps our first challenge. This means investing in developing relationships where trust can be fostered; environments where we can be appropriately vulnerable ourselves and create opportunities for others to share some of the areas they are working with in their own lives.

To allow these feelings of shame to surface where they can be seen for what they are, we need to come out of hiding. The first question in the Bible takes place in Genesis and is asked by God as he is looking for Adam and Eve in the garden. He asks simply, 'Where are you?'[77] Their shame had sent them away, hiding from God, and he comes looking for them. This is a wonderful picture of a God who longs for relationship with us.

Isn't it fascinating that the 'LORD God' comes to walk 'in the garden in the cool of the day'. This sounds like it was a regular occurrence. God is spending time with those he loved and created. Even though he is

---

77. Genesis 3:8-9.

the 'LORD God', busy running and sustaining the universe, let alone the world, he comes looking for Adam and Eve in the garden. This is our relational God doing what he does best, being in relationship with his creation. Spending time, or as a friend of mine, Rydal Hanbury, says 'wasting time with God', just hanging out.

God comes and walks in the garden, and I don't know if you've noticed, but there is something very different about the conversations you have when you are walking.

> There is something about walking and talking that's dissimilar to sitting for the dialogue. Maybe it's the full inclusion of our bodies, the lack of eye contact or what's culturally imbedded in our notions of safety. Maybe it's just being outside. Whatever the reason, one thing feels clear: when we walk and talk versus sit and talk, the quality of communication feels different.[78]

So writes David Baum, a conversation architect.

Baum's insights are helpful as we think not only about God's relationship with Adam and Eve, as he walked with them in the garden, but also our relationships with each other. He continues:

> The earliest root of the word 'walk' is 'well', meaning, 'to turn, bend, twist, roll,' and that is what walking and talking does. In the act of moving forward together, something in our nature is affected. If we're lucky, we can be reshaped or deepened by the conversations that happen when we move. If we are really lucky, we can be transformed.[79]

Shame enters the relationship that Adam and Eve have with God, because trust is broken. The serpent undermines the relationship by

---

78. David Baum, 'The Power of Walking Conversations', https://www.davidbaum.com/news/2018/2/4/the-power-of-walking-conversations (accessed 1.12.20).
79. Ibid.

sowing seeds of doubt. His words are subtle: 'did God really say...?'[80] This loss of trust that leads to uncertainty is what drives us to the secrecy, silence and judgement mentioned earlier as the three things on which shame thrives. Keeping things secret pushes us back behind our armour where we feel safe, and we don't have to trust anyone with our innermost thoughts and feelings. Adam and Eve's hiding in the garden is a direct outworking of the secrecy silence and judgement and, as we see here, is played out in a very physical way.

To quote Jordan Peterson:

> So here's a proposition: perhaps it is not simply the emergence of self-consciousness and the rise of our moral knowledge of Death and the Fall that besets us and makes us doubt our own worth. Perhaps it is instead our unwillingness – reflected in Adam's shamed hiding – to walk with God, despite our fragility and propensity for evil.[81]

Our hiding will sometimes have physical outworkings, as we may separate ourselves from a group of people or avoid contact and connection with some individuals. The underlying issue here is that shame tells us that there is something wrong with us, and this is discovered in the context of our relationships with others. We compare ourselves to other people and in doing so we see our inadequacy, we feel judged and we judge ourselves based on what we perceive is acceptable to the group. So, to avoid having these inadequacies confirmed over and over again, we hide those parts of ourselves that we are uncomfortable with from others.

> Removing shame requires more than forgiveness. Shame produces feelings of humiliation, disapproval, and abandonment. Shame means inadequacy of the entire person. While guilt says, 'I

---

80. Genesis 3:1.
81. Peterson, *12 Rules for Life: An Antidote to Chaos*, p. 57.

made a mistake'; shame says, 'I am a mistake.' Since the problem is the actual person, the shamed individual is banished from the group. To avoid such rejection and isolation, people mask their shame from others.[82]

Our challenge, then, should we choose to take it, is to both create and offer environments where we are accepted for who we are and don't feel judged. Where we feel safe and can learn to overcome the secrecy and silence that has kept us shut down in shame. The environments where this can happen need to have a good and healthy level of relational connection.

For this very reason, small groups will be the most likely place where this relational connection can take place. Small groups, if led well, create opportunities where trust can be built and genuine openness and vulnerability can be cultivated. They become places where we can be accepted for who we are and at the same time be encouraged to develop and grow beyond the limitations that we have built around ourselves for protection. In these atmospheres, we can start to experience love and acceptance from others.

For many of us, our evangelical faith background has encouraged us to ignore these inner places and feelings. It has told us not to trust them, and it has, for the large part, focused on the external activity rather than the 'inner journey'. So this will be a new pathway for some of us; one that we will need to discover and venture into with others. A more contemplative spirituality will serve us well in this endeavour too, one that gives us space and time to reflect and get in touch with the innermost places. In this way we stand a chance of seeing the defences we have built and getting in touch with the secrecy and silence that has held us captive.

---

82. Jayson Georges, *The 3D Gospel: Ministry in Guilt, Shame, and Fear Cultures* (Tim& 275 Press, 2014), Kindle edition, location 643-649.

Chapter 11: The Third Space

To engage in open conversations and allow communication to happen at a deeper level, rather than just trying to convince people of truth and win an argument, will need to be a skill that we all develop. Part of this will be a willingness to engage in the spiritual space that is opening up around us.

I have been reflecting on this for a while and use the phrase 'the third space' to describe what this might look like. This will involve us not being ashamed of our own spiritual traditions and being more creative and vulnerable about how we share our practices. So in this way it may be us as people of faith who need to overcome our shame, and come out of secrecy, silence and judgement. It will feel as if we need to be saved from this first in order to open up to others who are seeking.

The coffee shop chain Starbucks 'pioneered an idea they call "the third space"; the extra place people frequent after home and work.[83] In reality, this type of space has probably always existed. It was not so much the location but the concept that captured my imagination when I first heard the phrase 'the third space' several years ago. This is like many of my so-called new ideas, as yet again it is an adaptation of someone else's.

My mum and dad talk about the Lyon's Corner Houses: 'The first of the Lyon's teashops opened at 213 Piccadilly in 1894. Soon there were more than 250 white and gold fronted teashops occupying prestigious locations on many of London's high streets. Food and drink prices were the same in each teashop irrespective of locality and the tea was always the best available – although the Lyons blend was never sold or made

---

83. Anna van Praagh, *The Telegraph* June 2008, https://www.telegraph.co.uk/news/uknews/2131035/Starbucks-and-the-British-high-street.html (accessed 1.12.20).

available to the public.'[84] This was one of the third spaces of my parents' generation.

With this third space idea in mind, the question I started to explore was, what would a third space between the church community and those outside it look like? Let me explain the background to this question. For some time I have been conscious of a degree of discomfort around the idea of the church running outreach events that are sometimes packaged to disguise their true intent. So invitations to various 'how to' courses – parenting, marriage etc. – have what we might call hidden agendas, i.e. we really want people to find Jesus and follow him. On one such course a few years ago I was confronted by one of the participants with exactly that question: 'So, Trevor, I know this is being run by the church, so what is the hidden agenda?'

At about the same time, research done by the London Institute of Contemporary Christianity (LICC) entitled 'Beyond Belief' seemed to highlight something I had suspected for a while, which is that most people saw Christians as religious but not spiritual.[85] This was further confirmed whenever I stood in front of a secondary school class and heard how they thought of me as a Christian. They were confused – 'But, Sir,' (that's why I like going into schools, you get respect!), they would say, 'you're a Christian, you can't believe in spiritual things like angels and ghosts!' So not only are we viewed with suspicion as having hidden agendas, usually involving getting them into church and ultimately grabbing their money, but we are also seen as being religious – usually implying 'judgemental' and 'formulaic' and certainly not spiritual!

Many in the evangelical charismatic streams still live in the hope that one day the world will come and discover that we are indeed spiritual

84. Rob Baker, The Rise and Fall of the Lyons' Cornerhouses and their Nippy Waitresses, https://flashbak.com/the-rise-and-fall-of-the-lyons-cornerhouses-and-their-nippy-waitresses-35186 (accessed 1.12.20).
85. Nick Spencer, Beyond Belief?: Barriers and Bridges to Faith Today (London: LICC, 2004), p. 5.

as they turn up one Sunday morning and experience God amongst us. In reality, of course, this is increasingly less likely to happen, but praise God it will on some occasions.

So, what about the majority of people, how will they discover the reality of a spiritual dimension to life and the fact that the God we believe in not only exists but is passionate about them and wants to reveal himself to them? A God who empathises with them. They are most likely to discover the God we believe in through an encounter with us.

The other thing I have noted is the rising tide of spirituality in the culture around us. We are told that we have become a secular humanist culture, but I am not so sure that we are as far down that road as some would have us believe. The question raised in the school classroom, that I am spiritual and not just religious, does not question the existence of the spiritual realm; the students just don't associate spirituality with Christianity. This is largely because the New Age movement has popularised its own brand of spirituality. In research by both Steve Hollinghurst and Rob Frost, far from the secular worldview dominating the culture around us, we discover that spirituality is alive and well. In the introduction to the Essence course developed by Rob Frost, he writes:

> Whether we like it or not, New Age thinking and spirituality is now very much part of mainstream Western culture. The Henley Centre Report called 'The Paradox of Prosperity' indicates that around a quarter of all UK adults are currently seeking to renew their spiritual life. Every day thousands of people engage in activities which they see as 'spiritual'. Aromatherapy, personal development, green spirituality, astrology, tarot and alternative medicine are just a few of the activities which can become gateways into an exploration of spirituality.[86]

---

86. Rev Dr Rob Frost, *Essence* manual, Introduction, p. 4. PDF download available at https://www.sharejesusinternational.com/essence (accessed 1.12.20). Published: Eastbourne: Kingsway, 2002.

The problem is, as Spock from *Star Trek* might say, 'It's spiritual life, Jim, but not as we know it!' (For the Trekkies amongst you I know that Spock never actually said it.)

Another problem here, as if that's not enough already, is that many of us have grown up in very defensive church cultures. Here we are taught that we have to 'defend the truth'. We are contained in quite tight containers, particularly when it comes to spiritual experience. So, there is a whole list of things that we are told we should not be exposed to spiritually. The idea of getting tainted is very strong. From this background it is then hard to entertain the thought of connecting with an alternative spiritual culture. We just have loads of warning bells going off in our heads! I am highlighting this because some of the ideas that I am about to suggest may well set off these warning bells for you.

What is this third space about, then?

It is about having an intentionally spiritual space, not necessarily a place, but a space – somewhere where we as Christians can be seen to be spiritual. It's that simple. The crucial element here is that we are *seen*! That's why it needs to be a third space, i.e. outside of our church meetings and buildings. Also, much like the Starbucks idea, it needs to be an open space, by which I mean easy to connect with by anyone and everyone. It needs to be a level playing field, not a space where Christians tell others what to believe but a place of exploration, where we are not 'defending the truth' but rather letting the truth speak for itself amongst other views and ideas.

Relational spaces with spiritual atmospheres

Here is an example of a group that meets regularly aiming to create community and create a safe space for reflection, sharing about self-development and growing in self-awareness. Here we have been able to overcome the secrecy and silence that keeps us in shame. Our goal is to support each person on their path of development and as such we have naturally experienced empathy as we appreciate the unique contribution of each person, valuing those in whom we see similarities to ourselves and those who are different or have contrasting attributes. The heart of this group is to connect hearts and minds in intentional spirituality.

I have experienced first-hand the transforming nature of this group as it uses the personality tool called the Enneagram, which has grown in popularity recently in Christian circles as a diagnostic tool for spiritual formation. Thoughts and ideas of the early Christian Desert fathers and mothers can be seen, reflected in the Enneagram, particularly in overcoming barriers to contemplation and prayer.

I have been part of this group that has explored the inner journey and its development for a number of years. This Enneagram group has been skilfully led by a mature Christian friend, Jill Foulger,[87] who has created, with the help of this tool, a non-judgemental space where those joining us can talk openly about their inner challenges and, indeed, how these shape and affect their outer worlds and people they engage with.

I have been thinking about why this group has thrived and offered the safe space for us all to engage together. One of the keys here is that a level playing field is established through the description of the nine areas that are outlined as the Enneagram personality types. Each person self-identifies with a particular personality type description. This is very releasing, as you are not filling in a questionnaire or going through some sort of personality test and being 'told' who you should be. We discover these patterns through a comprehensive language that is inclusive of all cultures, nationality, religion and gender.

One of the things that makes the open sharing in the group possible, in my view, is that we can each talk about the personality type we most

---

87. Jill Foulger, counsellor and Enneagram teacher, https://www.counselling-hertfordshire.co.uk (accessed 7.5.21).

identify with and our lived experience. The framework provided by the Enneagram gives us a language and enables us to de-personalise what we share, to some degree, as it becomes a description of what it looks like for us. When others engage with us around our comments, they are talking about us and engaging with us, starting to understand where we are coming from, but all in the context of the personality type preference that we most identify with. This is helped further by those who share this particular personality type also talking about their experiences, so we do not feel alone or isolated, we share common experiences. In this way, we find companions on the journey, who relate to the sorts of things we have been experiencing but probably never talked about.

The depth of engagement in this group has been remarkable, and many of us have found levels of insight and health within ourselves and in relationships with others that have been amazing. This is just one example of a group that has created a space where secrecy, silence and judgement have started to be overcome, with significant personal growth as a result. There will be many ways in which these atmospheres can be created, so let's not hold back in exploring what might work in our particular context.

Chapter 12: Some Insights from Generation Y

A friend of mine, Andrea Campanale, who is also working with and researching the shame challenge, highlights another way of looking at what is going on with shame:

> Steve Pattison in his book *Shame: Theory, Therapy, Theology* comes up with an alternative. He suggests that in previous generations there were clear external constraints placed upon individuals by virtue of the role or place that they had in society. With this came prescribed expectations as to the appropriate behaviour that accompanied such a position and shame was conferred by the community upon those who transgressed these socially constructed boundaries of respectability.[88]

Andrea continues to unpack these ideas and very helpfully looks at how it impacts the way we think about ourselves:

> The present era perhaps deserves the description of being 'an age of shame' for ... If some modern sociological theorists are correct, we are living in the age of the self-conscious, reflective self. In this context, individuals conceive of themselves as being detached from traditional structures and relationships. When traditional roles, expectations and norms, together with the practices and rituals that support them, have fallen away, guilt associated with conforming to static, widely understood rules becomes less significant than the shame that accompanies uncertainty about the self in an-ever changing world.[89]

---

88. Andrea Campanale, 'A Gospel that Overcomes Shame' in eds Cathy Ross and Colin Smith, *Missional Conversations* (London: SCM Press, 2018), pp. 191-194.
89. Ibid.

What is being described here is the loss of the nomos as Berger describes it that we looked at earlier. Andrea goes on to describe something of the new nomos that has been created where the sense of self is thought of in terms our 'self-conscious' or 'reflective self'. A move from external to internal reference points:

> We have now moved to a situation where identity is no longer externally determined but dependent on our sense of self. There is a multiplicity of choices as to the persona we can adopt and having been largely set adrift from the constraints of needing to belong to a static, geographically rooted community, we can keep reinventing ourselves to ensure our face fits. Thus the alienation and rejection that is experienced as the manifestation of shame is now internalised and arises out of the anxiety that the image we are presenting is inauthentic and will be found out.[90]

We can see how this sense of inauthenticity works itself out in reality through a character called Lucy who is written about in an article on generation Y.[91] The article, by Tim Urban, caught my eye as I was thinking about shame and this generation in particular.

The article highlights the inner turmoil of the self-conscious, reflective self of Generation Y. It is written about 'Lucy' who is also part of a yuppie culture that makes up a large portion of Gen Y. It very cleverly looks at how Lucy, a typical Gen Y girl, feels about herself in relation to her peers and explores some of the presuppositions that she holds which create her perspectives. I have included a section here.

---

90. Stephen Pattison, *Shame: Theory, Therapy, Theology* (Cambridge: Cambridge University Press, 2008), p. 142.
91. Generation Y. Those born between the late 1970s and the mid-1990s.

Lucy … finds herself constantly taunted by a modern phenomenon: Facebook Image Crafting.

Social media creates a world for Lucy where A) what everyone else is doing is very out in the open, B) most people present an inflated version of their own existence, and C) the people who chime in the most about their careers are usually those whose careers (or relationships) are going the best, while struggling people tend not to broadcast their situation. This leaves Lucy feeling, incorrectly, like everyone else is doing really well, only adding to her misery:

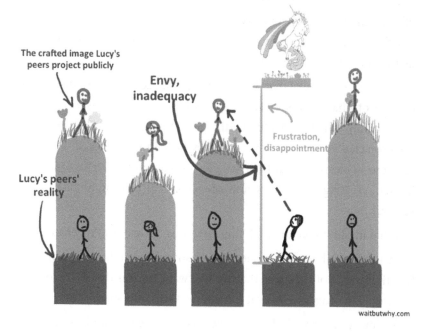

So that's why Lucy is unhappy, or at the least, feeling a bit frustrated and inadequate. In fact, she's probably started off her career perfectly well, but to her, it feels very disappointing.[92]

92. Tim Urban, 'Why Generation Y Yuppies Are Unhappy', 9 September 2013, https://waitbutwhy.com/2013/09/why-generation-y-yuppies-are-unhappy.html (accessed 8.12.20).

Lucy's envy of her peers drives her own sense of inadequacy, but as the diagram above so powerfully highlights each of Lucy's peers are in a similar place. I think this shows really well how social media is one of the components at play in creating and sustaining feelings of shame that result from us feeling less than we 'should be'.

What will ultimately break this sense of inadequacy which results in shame is engagement in real person-to-person relationships which allow Lucy and her peers to be honest about what is going on for them, and allows them to see for themselves the projected images they have created which ultimately keep them trapped in secrecy, silence and judgement. These are the spaces we need to create as Christian communities and offer to Lucy and her peers. We also need to recognize that it is not just Lucy's generation that is caught in this trap, as more and more of us are using and finding a sense of identity in this way.

The sense of envy that Lucy has can be described as discontent because of what someone else has got, or is doing. This leads to a sense of 'inadequacy' which is created by the peers themselves as they compare the projected images of themselves they have in turn created. What we see here so clearly is that their true feelings about themselves are well-hidden, creating the secrecy and silence that Brown highlights in her research.

What might it take to break this invidious circle of shame creation?

In light of what we have looked at so far, let's take some time to highlight some of the areas that we will want to consider as we look at the gospel message and how it can connect with our shame culture.

As you read through the next few chapters see which ideas resonate with you and think how they may be helpful in conversations you have about the gospel. Be mindful, of course, about where the individual, or indeed the group of people you are talking with, may be starting from. This implies that you have listened to them and heard a potential question or connection point.

Chapter 13: Jesus' Incarnation Linked to Empathy

Having thought about the context in which Jesus can be both encountered and talked about, we now move to what the message itself looks like, the words we might use, rather than the spaces they are communicated in. Shame thrives around three components, secrecy, silence and judgement. Let's remember Brené Brown's words:

> If you put shame in a Petri dish, it needs three ingredients to grow exponentially: secrecy, silence and judgment. If you put the same amount [of shame] in a Petri dish and douse it with empathy, it can't survive.[93]

The fact that the antidote to shame is empathy is indeed good news for us as we think about contextualising the gospel message into our shame culture. Jesus through his incarnation comes and lives amongst us as a real person, he inhabits 'our' very world. In doing this, he demonstrates complete empathy with us. He shares in the plight of our humanity even to the point of death; this is indeed total empathy.

Jesus' incarnation is something that has largely been linked to the Christmas story and is assigned to this season primarily. 'Immanuel … God with us,'[94] is contained in the Christmas box that comes out of the loft each year for December and then goes back again in the first few days of January. However, if empathy is the antidote to shame and Jesus shows his empathy with us through his incarnation, then this needs to be a 365-days-a-year celebration, as it is a core dimension to our gospel message as it relates to shame.

---

93. Brené Brown, TED Talk, 'Listening to Shame', March 2012, https://www.ted.com/talks/brene_brown_listening_to_shame (accessed 1.12.20).
94. Matthew 1:23.

Many people view God as disconnected from the reality of our world, a distant being who has no idea what it is like to live as we do. He is above and beyond us and is often thought of as being distant and aloof. Whilst, of course, in many senses this can be seen as true, God is indeed transcendent, he is also immanent. We have to some degree overemphasised the transcendence of God at the expense of his immanence. In modernity, we have depicted God as the one running the great machine, pulling the levers with little care for the consequences. Most of our church buildings with their towering ceilings and enormous doors are designed to display the majesty of God and tell us of his transcendence. We step in and feel tiny as the building looms above us.

He is, however, intimately connected to us, and our world: 'one God and Father of all, who is over all and through all and in all.'[95] 'He is before all things, and in him all things hold together.'[96] This, then, is not a God who has set the world running at creation and wandered off to attend to something else in the universe. This is a God who is intimately connected, who reveals his feelings about the world he has made and is sustaining.

One of my favourite verses of the Old Testament highlights this fact. 'The LORD saw that the human beings on the earth were very wicked and that everything they thought about was evil. He was sorry he had made human beings on the earth, and his heart was filled with pain.'[97] This is not the reaction of a distant, disconnected God, but one who is impacted by our actions, activity and the choices that drive them. The very heart of God that should be filled with love, in this description, from Genesis, is instead 'filled with pain'. He is experiencing the loss of relationship with the pinnacle of his creation, the very beings that he created with the capacity to love and be like him; he is now grieving

95. Ephesians 4:6.
96. Colossians 1:17.
97. Genesis 6:5-6, NCV.

as they choose to go their own way and live in independence from a relationship with him.

As a result of modernity we have, not surprisingly, minimised the element of 'partnering' when we think of Jesus. We have tended to reduce the gospel to a mechanistic vehicle for salvation. In this way we have focused on the mechanics of Jesus' death, and Jesus can tend to become the necessary sacrifice to appease God's wrath. The gospel message in this way takes on a transactional dynamic.

This very didactic approach has tended to make Jesus seem more like a necessary object than a person. This is something we need to redress. Having a person who empathises with us is, of course, a crucial part of the gospel as it applies to shame. This empathy is shown through participation and is demonstrated profoundly on the cross as we see Jesus suffering the depth of our human condition as he dies. We see God the Father's love for us and his connection to us and his world demonstrated so profoundly in the person of Jesus.

The incarnation is God's supreme act of grace - of participation, partnering, sharing - in the world afflicted by secondary causes.[98]

We can see how our perspectives need to change as we look at familiar verses through the eyes of shame and empathy. Take for instance Isaiah 53:4-5:

Surely he took up our pain and bore our suffering, yet we considered him punished by God, stricken by him, and afflicted. But he was pierced for our transgressions, he was crushed for our iniquities; the punishment that brought us peace was on him, and by his wounds we are healed.[99]

98. Bradley Jersak, *A More Christlike God* (Pasadena, CA: Plain Truth Ministries, 2015), p. 141.
99. Isaiah 53:4-5.

We have considered Jesus 'stricken' by God in our popular Western view of the atonement based on the idea of penal substitution. However when we look at these verses they say something contrary, in fact they actually say '*we* considered him punished by God, stricken by him and afflicted. But he was pierced for *our* transgressions'.[100] This happened at our hands, not God's! So can we perhaps read these verses differently in light of us thinking about making a connection to shame rather than guilt? In this way we move from Jesus needing to take our punishment for guilt to Jesus being one of us and in so doing going through the suffering of death.

> Moreover Jesus was actually bearing (carrying and enduring) the weight of our sin, our affliction and our infirmities. Jesus became a willing victim-participant in the human condition precisely in order to heal humanity of that very condition; the curse of sin and death.[101]

Notice the strength of Jersak's words: Jesus becomes a 'willing ... participant in the human condition'. This is empathy personified, it goes to the greatest extreme that empathy can go to; he steps fully into our broken world, and is tortured by us and eventually killed at our hands.

His blood was shed; the very lifeblood that courses through our veins ran through his. He identifies with our pain, shares our despair of life slipping away. As the writer of Hebrews puts it 'For surely it is not angels he helps, but Abraham's descendants. For this reason he had to be made like them, fully human in every way, in order that he might become a merciful and faithful high priest in service to God, and that he might make atonement for the sins of the people. Because he himself suffered when he was tempted, he is able to help those who are being tempted.'[102]

---

100. Emphasis mine.
101. Jersak, *A More Christlike God*, p. 142.
102. Hebrews 2:16-18.

To empathise with our human condition, Jesus is obedient to the terms of his incarnation as he becomes so fully human that he is able to die, 'And being found in appearance as a man, he humbled himself by becoming obedient to death – even death on a cross!'[103] As the context of this passage is Jesus coming and dwelling among us in human likeness, it seems possible to interpret these verses as applying to his being obedient to his humanity, as we all are in our human condition. In this way we connect to the empathy of Jesus being like us which is more relevant in the shame context rather than the perhaps more familiar interpretation that he was being obedient to God his Father.

Whilst I am sure both outcomes can be implied from the passage, I think the assertion that he is obedient to his human condition is very compelling when we are thinking about Jesus empathising with us in our humanity.

'For we do not have a high priest who is unable to empathize with our weaknesses, but we have one who has been tempted in every way, just as we are – yet he did not sin.'[104]

---

103. Philippians 2:8.
104. Hebrews 4:15, NIV (US).

Chapter 14: Leaving One Community and Forming Another

Jesus leaves his glorious position in the family of the Trinity

Let's spend a few moments and look at some verses from Philippians.

> In your relationships with one another, have the same mindset as Christ Jesus: who, being in very nature God, did not consider equality with God something to be used to his own advantage; rather, he made himself nothing by taking the very nature of a servant, being made in human likeness.And being found in appearance as a man, he humbled himself by becoming obedient to death – even death on a cross![105]

Shame excludes and separates us; it produces feelings of being 'less than' others. Jesus experiences this as he leaves the Trinity and takes on the 'nature of a servant'. He does not 'count equality with God' something to hold onto but gives it up. Making himself 'nothing': what an empty term – the one who was everything becomes nothing. This resonates so much with what shame does, it devalues and denigrates who we are and makes us feel as if we are nothing. We can feel worthless and abandoned. So, Jesus leaves his glorious status behind and enters our world.

Paintings and pictures of Jesus do not readily depict this image as they have a tendency to restore his glory by showing his shining clothes, and often portray him with a halo and glowing shimmer of light around him. We find it difficult to imagine that the Jesus thus depicted was capable of feeling all the emotions we encounter.

---

105. Philippians 2:5-8.

The relational separation for all members of the Trinity is not something we often dwell on; their sense of loss as Jesus empties himself and is born amongst us. This sense of separation and resulting loss of value and status is a fundamental component of the shame dilemma. To know that we have a Godhead who experienced this first-hand will be of great comfort as we all reflect on our own sense of isolation and loss, of somehow being less than we know we could be or desire to become.

He is born in a humble and vulnerable state here on earth and identifies with our frailty

He grew up before him like a tender shoot, and like a root out of dry ground. He had no beauty or majesty to attract us to him, nothing in his appearance that we should desire him. He was despised and rejected by mankind, a man of suffering, and familiar with pain. Like one from whom people hide their faces he was despised, and we held him in low esteem.[106]

These verses from Isaiah move us from looking at Jesus' change of relationship within the Trinity to his experience of being on the edge of the society that he was born into. He knows what it is like to be despised and rejected. He does not join the elite and look for honour, prestige and status. He is at odds with the social structures of his day and is critical of the false status that is given through them. The strength of this is shown in the phrase, 'Like one from whom people hide their faces'.

The passage paints a picture of Jesus in his full humanity, 'a man of suffering, and familiar with pain'. Unlike many of the paintings of Jesus which, as I previously remarked, show him radiant, pristine and glorious, these verses describe him as 'despised and rejected', words that resonate with shame; '... held him in low esteem' – of little value,

---

106. Isaiah 53:2-3.

which is yet another aspect that shame wallows in. So, Jesus in his frailty becomes vulnerable and identifies with our humanity; he experiences it first-hand.

In his full humanity he receives the Father's honour

'And a voice from heaven said, "This is my Son, whom I love; with him I am well pleased."'[107]

Jesus hears the voice of his Father as he is baptised by John in the Jordan. This affirmation from God the Father comes at the very beginning of Jesus' ministry; it affirms him not based on what he has done or will do, but on who he is – 'This is my Son'. In his full humanity, Jesus pleases God the Father. Just as in the creation account in Genesis God says our creation as male and female was 'very good',[108] so here God the Father affirms Jesus' humanity and is 'well pleased'.

God does not hate our humanity, as some would have us believe, or despise us because of it, he celebrates it. Both in Genesis as he creates us, and in the person of Jesus. This is indeed good news. That is not to say that God celebrates all that we sometimes choose to become or the outrageous things we may do, but he is for us and on our side as we seek to live as his followers in our fully human state.

I encountered this truth in a very personal way when I was speaking at a local church on the topic of the gospel message and shame. We had a time of discussion at the end of my talk in which I opened the floor up for questions and observations. We had a very fruitful time interacting together. As is my custom on these occasions, I used a microphone and go with it to people who want to comment from their seat, rather than ask them to come to the front. Towards the end of our discussion, I was stood next to Roy, who I had known for a number of years and until

---

107. Matthew 3:17.
108. Genesis 1:26-31.

recently had led the church I was speaking in. He turned to me and said, 'Just as a tree gives glory to God by being a tree, so you, Trevor … give glory to God by being Trevor.'[109] I was so moved as these words were spoken over me. It had never occurred to me that I could simply give glory to God by being who he had created me to be. Roy went on to say that this was not his idea but one he had borrowed from Thomas Merton. As you can imagine, I looked this up when I got home and here it is:

> A tree gives glory to God by being a tree. For in being what God means it to be, it is obeying him. It 'consents,' so to speak, to his creative love. It is expressing an idea which is in God and which is not distinct from the essence of God, and therefore a tree imitates God by being a tree. The more a tree is like itself, the more it is like him. If it tried to be like something else which it was never intended to be, it would be less like God.[110]

There was a real sense of relief that I was somehow OK, it was all right to be me. God understood what it was like; he knew because he had made me to be me. It sounds so obvious now, but it really hit me in the moment and something shifted within me as those words were spoken. It is also interesting to note that Roy had status in this Christian community as he had until recently led them; also he was someone I looked up to. This made his words even more significant to me and, as a result, had greater effect on my sense of being valued for who I am. In this way my internal voices that gave the shame talk were silenced and a greater feeling of value was bestowed on me, both by God's delight in me being who he has created me to be, and in this being delivered by Roy in person in the way that he did.

---

109. Roy Gregory, Ashley Church, St Albans, February 2019. Used with permission.
110. Thomas Merton, *New Seeds of Contemplation* (London: Hollis & Carter, 1949), https://www.goodreads.com/quotes/8644395-a-tree-gives-glory-to-god-by-being-a-tree (accessed 8.12.20).

He includes as his friends those who are rejected by the social structures of his day

'Jesus was killed because of the way he ate.' You'd be hard-pressed to find a 'cooler' soundbite about the Gospels than that statement by New Testament scholar Robert Karris. I so wish I'd thought of it first.

So writes Conrad Gempf in *Mealtime Habits of the Messiah*.[111]

When the teachers of the law who were Pharisees saw him eating with the sinners and tax collectors, they asked his disciples: 'Why does he eat with tax collectors and sinners?' On hearing this, Jesus said to them, 'It is not the healthy who need a doctor, but those who are ill. I have not come to call the righteous, but sinners.'[112]

These people were seen as 'sinners' because they were rejected by the social structures of the day. They were made to feel unworthy and unwanted. Jesus includes them because they are the very people he wants to help find wholeness and acceptance. 'It is not the healthy who need a doctor, but those who are ill,'[113] he says.

Jesus knows long before Brené Brown's research that the antidote to shame is empathy, so he draws alongside them, shares their lives, eats with them, which is the greatest sign of friendship and empathy. He is not just an acquaintance. He is a real friend. He risks being counted amongst them, and in so doing, bringing shame on himself. In being seen to identify with them he risks being included with them in their exclusion. This is of no significance to him compared with how he feels about their inclusion in his kingdom.

---

111. Conrad Gempf, *Mealtime Habits of the Messiah* (Grand Rapids, MI: Zondervan, 2005), p. 18. Original source of Karris' statement unknown.
112. Mark 21:16-17.
113. Matthew 9:12.

Simon Cozens writes:

> I was surprised when I realised how much of Jesus teaching has
> to do with the way in which the world's shame system operates.
> So much of what he says is about the way we make judgements
> of one another, and about our desire to curate our identities to
> impress others and gain their approval.[114]

This tells us something about Jesus' own sense of identity; its source is
not found in the earthly structures that dominate his day. Even though
he is somehow separated from the Father as he has left the glory of
heaven, he still carries the inner identity of his personhood as a member
of the Trinity. From this centre he goes about establishing his kingdom
'on earth as it is in heaven.'[115]

He is seeking to bring about the relationships that he knows we were
all designed to flourish in, the very relationships that he refers to time
and again that he has with the Father and the Spirit. His aim, as John so
profoundly records in his Gospel, is that 'I will not leave you as orphans;
I will come to you. Before long, the world will not see me any more, but
you will see me. Because I live, you also will live. On that day you will
realise that I am in my Father, and you are in me, and I am in you.'[116]

---

114. Simon Cozens, *Looking Shame in the Eye* (London: IVP, 2019), p. 73.
115. Matthew 6:10.
116. John 14:18-20.

Chapter 15: Life in All its Fullness

I heard it said recently that our favourite verses in the Bible tell us a lot about ourselves. I have always liked John 10:10 where Jesus says, 'I have come that they may have life, and have it to the full.' Those who know me well will tell you that I indeed like to live life to the full, sometimes too full! So much of what we seem to offer as Christians feels a lot less than life to the full to me! This fullness of life, in my view, needs to be a very real part of what the gospel offers.

Jesus' healing miracles reinstate previously excluded people

Physical disfigurement was seen as a punishment for sin, hence the questions often asked in this regard around Jesus' healing miracles, as we see from this passage: 'His disciples asked him, 'Rabbi, who sinned, this man or his parents, that he was born blind?'[117] Jesus goes on to answer that neither the man nor his parents sinned to cause this.

People with physical issues were seen as unholy and kept at a distance, they were shamed because there was something inherently wrong with them. Their disease or disorder was seen as a sign of judgement by God caused by some previous sin, in this case, by them or maybe a parent. Jesus, however, shows compassion and includes them through conversation and touch, at the risk of defiling himself. Jesus does more than including them himself as he reaches out and touches them and welcomes them; he also ensures that others accept and receive them. To do this he heals them, which removed the impediment that made them unclean and caused their shame, as far as society was concerned, so they were no longer defined by their illness.

---

117. John 9:2.

In this way Jesus pushes back the kingdom of darkness with its earthly power structures that seek to 'kill and destroy'[118] people through exclusion, and he sets them free, reinstating them into the social order of the day. In so doing, he does two things: firstly, he pushes against the recognised structures as he reaches out to the people belittled and ostracised by them, and secondly he works with the structures as he heals people, so they can be included. So, we see here a double transformation. Firstly, there is the transformation that happens as Jesus reaches out to these excluded individuals and shows them value through his friendship and inclusion. Secondly, there is the transformation that happens through the physical change and restoration of their bodies, showing that God is concerned for our physical well-being. He values highly our physical world and the place that we have in it. So, just as Jesus knows his identity as a son and this shapes the way he interacts with others and the world around him, so the same is true of us, as sons and daughters of God the Father. A theme that Paul picks up in Romans as he writes:

> I consider that our present sufferings are not worth comparing with the glory that will be revealed in us. For the creation waits in eager expectation for the children of God to be revealed. For the creation was subjected to frustration, not by its own choice, but by the will of the one who subjected it, in hope that the creation itself will be liberated from its bondage to decay and brought into the freedom and glory of the children of God. We know that the whole creation has been groaning as in the pains of childbirth right up to the present time. Not only so, but we ourselves, who have the firstfruits of the Spirit, groan inwardly as we wait eagerly for our adoption to sonship, the redemption of our bodies.[119]

---

118. John 10:10.
119. Romans 8:18-23.

In this way we pick up Jesus' mandate to see the healing of our world as we participate in 'hope that the creation itself will be liberated from its bondage to decay and brought into the freedom and glory of the children of God'. We are indeed those children, adopted into God's family to continue the work of Jesus to see his kingdom come through our care of creation.

His life is one of rejection by the earthy powers of a shameful culture that excluded people

Jesus risked exclusion and rejection as he engaged with those who were themselves excluded, and we see the somewhat inevitable outcomes of his actions as he is indeed rejected and ridiculed and eventually killed by the earthly power constructs. It should come as no surprise to us that this happens. The very fact that Jesus is bringing his kingdom in means that there is an existing kingdom already in place that his kingdom has to overthrow. That is to say, that his kingdom stands against an existing one that is in place. This is often a hard concept for us to convey as our Western culture, unlike many others, has diminished the place of the spiritual to such a degree that there is little if any concept of this sort of cosmic battle.

A recent conversation with a friend serving in the UK as a missionary from Hong Kong highlighted this. In her post-Alpha course small group, she was amazed to discover that people didn't believe in the devil, Satan, or any of the dark forces that would be associated with him. For her, these were givens; from her worldview, the work of evil forces on the earth was obvious and as a result, the battle we find ourselves caught up in as Christians. Not so for many in her group as they discussed the topic. She was really shocked and we had a long conversation, discussing how this could be the case. One helpful way I have found to see how this operates is through the reflections of Dr Paul Hiehbert.

Reflecting on his experience as a missionary in India, Heihbert comes to the realisation that his training as a scientist in the West led him to deal with the world through an empirical lens. This he found was at odds with his experience and theological reference as a missionary in India.[120] He observed a three-tier worldview in Indian which Wimber labels as follows;

1. Transcendent world beyond ours
2. Supernatural forces on this earth
3. Empirical world of our senses[121]

Heighbert noticed that the dominant worldview in the West had only two dimensions, as the middle one had been removed. The effects of us embracing the Enlightenment and the onset of modernity, with its basis set in the empirical world of our senses, had no place for the supernatural. Wimber lists as follows some of the features of this missing section:

Spirits, ghosts, ancestors, demons

Earthly gods and goddesses that live within trees, hills, rivers and villages

Supernatural forces; planetary influences, evil eyes, power of magic, sorcery etc

Holy Spirit, angels, demons, Signs and Wonders, gifts of the Spirit[122]

The loss of this reality has had a number of effects on the way we in the West view the world that we live in. I just want to focus on one here, as it impacts the area we are looking at. The loss of this middle section

---

120. Paul Hiehbert, 'Flaw of the Excluded Middle', *Missiology*, January 1982, pp 35-47.
121. John Wimber, *Power Evangelism* (London: Hodder & Stoughton, 1985), p. 86.
122. For a fuller explanation of this insight, see Wimber, *Power Evangelism*, pp. 82-88.

and what it represents in terms of the supernatural at work in our world has meant that we have lost the on-earth reality of the conflict between kingdoms that we are caught up in. One of the results of this is that we have little or no concept of any form of evil as the New Testament would understand it.

Or, to put it another way, as a friend of mine describes it 'the devil has gone missing'.[123] Jesus steps into our world to establish a kingdom at odds with that of Satan. A world built around the constructs of false identity made outside of a relationship with our creator God.

Jesus is very aware of these schemes and sets out to thwart them. He knows that 'The thief comes only to steal and kill and destroy'; he, on the other hand, has come 'that they may have life, and have it to the full'.[124] Once we recognise, as John Woolmer points out, that the devil has indeed 'gone missing', it starts to make sense of some of the things we run into. If God is indeed distant and unconcerned, as we pointed out earlier, and if we don't believe in an evil force (whatever name we might use to describe this), it stands to reason that the person who gets the blame for everything is this uncaring, disconnected, distant God of ours! So we have a task to do here in re-establishing a biblical worldview that helps us to see the world as Jesus encountered it. The person who wants to keep us out of relationship with each other and with the God we were designed to work in partnership with is indeed the devil – in whatever way we might understand him or want to describe him to our twenty-first-century audience. As Paul points out:

> As for you, you were dead in your transgressions and sins, in which you used to live when you followed the ways of this world and of the ruler of the kingdom of the air, the spirit who is now at work in those who are disobedient.[125]

---

123. For more on this topic, see John Woolmer, *The Devil Goes Missing?* (Oxford: Lion Hudson, 2017).
124. John 10:10.
125. Ephesians 2:1-2.

It is this power that is at work in the world that Jesus lived in, that set itself against him and his ways of working. One of its weapons was, and still is, shame that keeps us out of relationship with each other and God. This is what Jesus came to save us from and he makes this clear in his manifesto:

> The Spirit of the Lord is on me, because he has anointed me to proclaim good news to the poor. He has sent me to proclaim freedom for the prisoners and recovery of sight for the blind, to set the oppressed free, to proclaim the year of the Lord's favour.[126]

I have found the work of Greg Boyd helpful in understanding something of this lost aspect of our worldview. In particular his work *Satan and the Problem of Evil*.[127]

126. Luke 4:18-19.
127. Gregory A. Boyd, *Satan and the Problem of Evil* (Downers Grove, IL: IVP, 2001).

Chapter 16: God's Cruciform Nature

Jesus' shameful death on a cross as a result of his loving and inclusive nature

> It's time for Christianity to rediscover the real Biblical theme of *restorative justice,* which focuses on rehabilitation, healing and reconciliation, not punishment. We should call Jesus' story the 'myth of redemptive suffering' – not as in 'paying a price' but as in offering the self for the other. 'At-one-ment' instead of atonement![128]

As we described earlier, Jesus goes to the cross not necessarily because God the Father needs him to as a way of being an offering for our sin, which is the way we would think about it as his death relates to our guilt. But rather, that he lives a life that is so countercultural that he needs to be excluded and killed to ensure that the status quo is upheld: in thinking in this way we are looking through the lens of shame. This status quo, of course, has larger connotations than we may have imagined in light of our earlier explorations around the nature of the forces at work here on the earth!

This means that Jesus dies a shameful death as one who is ostracised. In this way, he once again shows his empathy with us and in particular, with those who suffer at the hands of those with power in our world. The criminal death that he suffers is out of a desire to see his kingdom come as he radically establishes a new order in the way he carries out relationships, which is in direct opposition to the power constructs of his day.

His challenge through his death turns the known norms of his day on their head. He puts himself at the mercy of this world and in the hands

---

128. Richard Rohr, *The Universal Christ: How a Forgotten Reality Can Change Everything We See, Hope For and Believe* (London: SPCK, 2019), pp. 141-142.

of his Father and is prepared to take the extreme path of identifying with our human condition by experiencing the depths of our humanity as he suffers and dies as one of us. 'Greater love has no one than this: to lay down one's life for one's friends.'[129] So we can see his death as an ultimate act of empathy with us; it is part of what makes him totally human, that he embraces fully the life that we lead, including suffering and death.

This is the cruciform nature of the kingdom of God that

Jesus inaugurated, consider the humble, loving and countercultural way Jesus interacted with people. The cruciform love that eventually led Jesus to enter into solidarity with sinners and to appear as a guilty criminal on Calvary was already leading him to enter into solidarity with sinners to appear as one of them through his ministry.

Jesus scandalously fellowshipped with prostitutes, tax collectors, and others who were harshly judged by the religious establishment of his day ... He broke religious taboos by interacting with, and even touching, people who were viewed as unclean and whom the OT law prohibited touching ... And Jesus rebelled against the patriarchal social structure of his day by interacting with women – even women with shameful pasts – in respectful ways.[130]

The upside down, inside out nature of the kingdom of God that Jesus demonstrates through these acts of inclusion and identification put him on a collision course with the authorities of his day. A course that would lead to his death.

The loving way Jesus interacted with, and spoke about, people who most Jews despised – e.g., Samaritans, Gentiles, and Roman

129. John 15:13.
130. Gregory Boyd, *Cross Vision* (Minneapolis, MN: Fortress Press, 2018), p. 43.

centurions – was scandalous, to say the least ... In all these ways, Jesus was sacrificially resisting racial prejudices within his culture, and as is true of every other aspect of Jesus's ministry, this aspect culminates on the cross. For the cross reveals God stooping an unsurpassable distance and paying an unsurpassable price to ascribe unsurpassable worth to every human form every tribe and nation throughout history.[131]

This re-valuing of every human being is incredible and at the heart of the message of Jesus' life as a whole, and the cross in particular.

Jesus experiences shame as Peter denies knowing him. This rejection of friendship and refusal to acknowledge any connection to Jesus by Peter is profound as we think of it in the context of shame. 'He denied it again, with an oath: 'I don't know the man!''[132]

Jesus is scourged, and spat on,[133] belittled by his mockers – all things that induce feelings of shame and an overwhelming sense of being worthless. His few possessions are taken from him and he is stripped naked, reminding us of Adam and Eve's first feelings of shame in the garden. From the cross, he cries out in desperation, 'My God, my God, why have you forsaken me?'[134]

His overcoming of these earthly and heavenly suppressive powers through his resurrection

And having disarmed the powers and authorities, he made a public spectacle of them, triumphing over them by the cross.[135]

This is such a great verse from Colossians; the letter is so Jesus-focused. This is the 'Christus Victor' theme that focuses on Christ's triumph

---

131. Ibid.
132. Matthew 26:72.
133. Matthew 26:67.
134. Matthew 27:46.
135. Colossians 2:15.

over death and over the 'powers and authorities' mentioned in the verses above.

It is often interpreted as referring to powers in a cosmic sense, i.e. those outside of the realm of our earthly existence. For the situation we are working with here, where our shame dynamic is earthed in the reality of relationships here and now, we need to apply these and other verses like them in a less cosmic and more earthly way. So the 'powers and authorities' are those manifestly evident in our everyday lives. In this way we can see the 'Christus Victor' theme being played out on an earthly stage and connected to the narrative of the rest of Jesus' life – if you like, a continuation of the encounters that he has already been having through his earthly ministry.

J. Denny Weaver coins the phrase 'Narrative Christus Victor' as a way of describing this view. One writer reflecting on Weaver's work sets it in the context of other atonement theories in this way:

It bears some resemblance to the 'cosmic battle' version of Christus Victor, but it brings the battle down from the cosmos and locates it first of all in the confrontation between Jesus and the forces of evil embodied, for example, in the Roman Empire that executed him.

Weaver's God is free to forgive without the mechanistic constraints of honour, holiness, or retributive justice. Jesus' victory is seen not in a violent murder that God needs, but in Jesus' life of freedom from the powers and his exposure of their true nature and ultimate weakness in his faithfulness unto death and resurrection. Understood this way, the atonement becomes a model for discipleship, for following Jesus in the ways of peace and trusting in God's victorious love.[136]

---

136. Ted Grimsrud, 'Reflections on J. Denny Weaver's *The Nonviolent Atonement*, https:// peacetheology.files.wordpress.com/2011/10/atla0001746158.pdf (accessed 8.12.20)

So, as we can see, this lends itself very well to the context of shame. Firstly, it takes the 'Christus Victor' idea and lands it in an earthly realm. It is this earthly realm that is the relational stage for the power play which sets up the structures that exclude and cause shame. Secondly, it links Jesus' death and resurrection to his life, making them a continuation of his ministry rather than somehow a separate act that brings about salvation. Thirdly, as Grimsrud highlights, the atonement set in this way becomes 'a model for discipleship, for following Jesus in the ways of peace and trusting in God's victorious love'.

So Jesus, through his resurrection, obtains victory over the very things that hold us captive in this world. This new life he offers has its focus on the here and now to enable us to live as Jesus lived, and to live as those who know the resurrection power that raised him from the dead which enables us to live like him, by 'trusting in [his] victorious love'.

Putting our trust in this 'victorious love' sets the context of our salvation in a very relational way. Trust is built through relational engagement; it comes as we push against the tendency of shame to isolate us and in so doing, not enabling us to build relational trust.

As people who live in this reality we are indeed new creations, living not in isolation from God and others as shame dictates, but living out lives that demonstrate trusting relationships that resonate with those demonstrated by our Trinitarian God. We are no longer captive to our own egos, bound by earthly constraints, but called to live lives that are outrageously free. We can then say along with Paul: 'For in Christ all the fullness of the Deity lives in bodily form, and in Christ you have been brought to fullness. He is the head over every power and authority.'[137]

---

137. Colossians 2:9-10.

We become new creations

Becoming someone new and different is very appealing if we live with shame. We have an opportunity to start again. To get rid of the old person who we loathed and thought of as useless and worthless and can become a new person. 'If I see the gospel in terms of guilt where I am fine but what *I've done* is a problem, then being put to death is not a very appealing offer. I quite like being me; I just want my debts paid, thank you very much.'[138] We can see how this approach is often taken with the 'wrongdoing' idea and how discipleship takes a second place in this sort of thinking; no real change is required here, just a forgiveness transaction. I can simply add Christianity to who I am.

> But if my problem is shame, if the problem is that *I* am wrong, then dying to self sounds like something I really need right now. I don't want there to be continuity between who I was before I met Christ and who I am afterwards – I turned to Christ precisely because I wanted to get rid of that old stuff.[139]

In this way, the old person who was filled with shame has gone and a new person has been born. To use Jesus' familiar words to Nicodemus: 'You must be born again.'[140] It makes so much more sense when we think of it in the shame context. Being born again has the ideas attached to it of discovering afresh who we are, this time as God's children, shaped by all that he thinks of us rather than of the world's shaping and thinking that formed our old selves. As we will see later, this re-birth does not happen in isolation but we are formed as members of a new community and together we discover our new identity as part of a new family.

The idea of us becoming new creations has both horizontal as well as vertical dimensions to it. Our personalities, characters and our identities

---

138. Cozens, *Looking Shame in the Eye*, p. 101.
139. Ibid.
140. John 3:7.

are shaped by those around us. This shaping will not stop happening as we become new creations; although there will be a transformational encounter with God that will initiate the new person, and in that sense, bring the vertical dimension alive. There will also need to be the horizontal connections that help to form this newly created life. The early Church set up its Catechism with exactly that in mind to ensure that the new Christians became new creations.[141] John Wesley established similar patterns through his Bands and Classes for this very purpose of discipleship.

Similarly, when we look at other verses that pick up this theme, they take on a new dimension when viewed through the lens of shame: 'Therefore, if anyone is in Christ, the new creation has come: 'the old has gone, the new is here!'[142] This is so much more than the old metaphors that we would have associated with this in the more legal constructs of having 'the slate wiped clean'. This is so much more dramatic when viewed through the eyes of shame. It's as if the slate itself has been replaced, not just wiped clean so more things can be written on it. All associations with what was there before have gone, the transformation is total and the new is unrecognisable as against the old. This is totally necessary to deal with the shame idea.

'We were therefore buried with him through baptism into death in order that, just as Christ was raised from the dead through the glory of the Father, we too may live a new life.'[143] Our baptism symbolises this death of the shameful self and we symbolically kill off the old shame-filled person as we go down into the water and rise as a new creation empowered by Christ to live a new life where shame will no longer hold dominion over us.

---

141. For insights into this topic, see Alan Kreider, *The Change of Conversion and the Origin of Christendom* (New York: Continuum International Publishing Group – Trinity, 1999).
142. 2 Corinthians 5:17.
143. Romans 6:4.

Chapter 17: The Place of the Ascension

Jesus' acceptance back into the family of the Trinity through his ascension

In my experience, the ascension has never been a key part of our gospel message. The fact that Jesus ascends is not a critical component in the ways we have thought about our salvation. When we are looking through the eyes of shame, however, I think the ascension takes on a different light. We mentioned earlier that in leaving the Trinity and coming to live amongst us, Jesus experiences in some sense, separation and loss of relationship; could this be a link to what we experience as loss of relationship through shame? Jesus himself puts it this way: 'I came from the Father and entered the world; now I am leaving the world and going back to the Father.'[144]

His ascension allows him to return to the Father; this re-inclusion in the Trinitarian community is what finally overcomes the shame that Jesus has carried. We can think of Jesus potentially carrying shame in a number of ways. Jesus has 'emptied himself',[145] as expressed in Philippians 2, and in so doing became 'nothing';[146] this is the word *ekenosen*, from *kenosis* or 'emptying'. We have to be careful how we work with these verses as they are complex and have a great number of different interpretations, and as such are often fraught with controversy.

In whatever way we think Jesus 'empties himself', it is the place that many in our culture find themselves, feeling exactly that; they have little or no value and are simply nothing. He is described in verse 7 as being a servant. Jesus has lived on the margins of society, being misunderstood, despised and rejected. He has died a shameful death partly as a result

---

144. John 16:28
145. Philippians 2:7, NRSV.
146. ESV.

of including those in his company who were themselves outcasts. Not to mention the fact that he posed a real threat to the authorities who were concerned about upholding the structures that kept people in their shame. He is rescued by his Father as he is resurrected through the power of the Holy Spirit and is then reunited with the Father and honoured by him as he is glorified at his right hand (Mark 16:19). We could suggest here that his separation and shame are overcome through his welcome back to the community of the Trinity as he ascends.

We need to remember of course, that Jesus was not completely separated from the Father and the Holy Spirit whilst he was on earth, until his death, although the nature of that relationship was different. An area that would benefit form more reflection and thought as we think about how we connect with the shame idea.

What happens in the ascension is that he re-joins this Trinitarian community. So we can see this as part of the story of our salvation in that it shows us that Jesus is welcomed back into the community of the Trinity. He tells his disciples not to hold onto him: 'Do not hold on to me, for I have not yet ascended to the Father. Go instead to my brothers and tell them, "I am ascending to my Father and your Father, to my God and your God."'[147]

What is really 'good news' about these verses is that the disciples are included in. Jesus is ascending to his Father and their Father. Through believing in him, they also have been accepted as children of the Father. This is, of course, a key part of the gospel message.

Therefore, since we have a great high priest who has ascended into heaven, Jesus the Son of God, let us hold firmly to the faith we profess. For we do not have a high priest who is unable to empathize with our weaknesses, but we have one who has been tempted in every way, just as we are – yet he did not sin. Let us

147. John 20:17.

then approach God's throne of grace with confidence, so that we may receive mercy and find grace to help us in our time of need.[148]

There is so much we could draw out of these verses from Hebrews. I want to just make two observations here as we think about Jesus' ascension and how it connects to our gospel that overcomes shame. The first is that we have Jesus the man who has ascended to heaven; in the same way we are not excluded from connection with God as humans and in this way we to need to 'hold firmly' to the faith we have. He acts on our behalf, being a high priest for us in this throne room. He can do this on our behalf because he is one of us, he 'empathize[s] with our weaknesses'.

Secondly, we can approach God's 'throne of grace' not timidly and apologetically as we would if we were carrying our shame, rather we can come 'with confidence'! Not out of arrogance or pride, however, but in humility to 'receive mercy and find grace ... in our time of need.'

Similarly, Paul writes to the church at Ephesus:

And God raised us up with Christ and seated us with him in the heavenly realms in Christ Jesus, in order that in the coming ages he might show the incomparable riches of his grace, expressed in his kindness to us in Christ Jesus. For it is by grace you have been saved, through faith – and this is not from yourselves, it is the gift of God – not by works, so that no one can boast. For we are God's handiwork, created in Christ Jesus to do good works, which God prepared in advance for us to do.[149]

There are a number of things going on here, which I want to draw attention to. Notice how the resurrection and ascension are connected together not just for Jesus but for us as well: 'And God raised us up with Christ and seated us with him in the heavenly realms in Christ Jesus'.

---

148. Hebrews 4:14-16, NIV (US).
149. Ephesians 2:6-10.

This is a dimension we have generally overlooked; we talk in terms of being raised on the last day but actually this is current, and reflects what has happened rather than what will happen. So there is a dimension here that is not futuristic, which we often think of it as being, i.e. one day we will reign with Christ, but rather 'God has raised us up with Christ' and just as he ascended so we have also ascended and are seated with him!

Another area I want to draw our attention to, which is reflected here, is anchoring us back to the idea that we are being made by God as his 'handiwork'. This re-telling of the 'creation of us' is now as a result of us being 'created in Christ Jesus' – our identity is re-purposed. Once, human beings were in union with God as his creations, and in him we found our identity as he walked with us in the garden, as described in Genesis. This was lost as we looked for our independence and moved away from that defining relationship. Now that identity here is rediscovered through our recreation in Christ Jesus.

In this way we are drawn into the Trinitarian relationship as we are 'seated' with Christ. This is all made possible because of the ascension. If Christ had not ascended then we would not be able to be seated with him. One proof of our recreation is that we are seated with him. The Amplified version puts it like this: 'For we are His workmanship [His own master work, a work of art], created in Christ Jesus [reborn from above – spiritually transformed, renewed, ready to be used] for good works, which God prepared [for us] beforehand [taking paths which He set], so that we would walk in them [living the good life which He prearranged and made ready for us].'[150] I particularly like the 'ready to be used' part; this restores our sense of purpose, which has been lost for so many of us. It reinstates us as being valuable to God, confirmed by the fact that he is choosing to use us in his purposes – as partakers of, and active participants in, seeing his kingdom come on earth as it is in heaven.

---

150. Ephesians 2:10, AMP.

The final words of Jesus in his farewell discourse in John chapters 14-16 show how the ascension is a vital component in Jesus' thinking around what he has come to do. He has to convince the disciples that it is necessary for him to return to the Father, and he takes three chapters to achieve this with them.

The Son being glorified as he returns to the Father is ultimately what releases the Spirit to come and fill us. Without Jesus returning to the Father, this outpouring would not happen, with the result that the work he had started on earth would not continue. We become his body as we are filled with his Spirit, and as this happens we become new creations in the context of the body of believers.

This is indeed good news for us – our very nature is recreated as the Holy Spirit comes and lives in us. This in itself is an act of empathy, and is yet another expression of his love for us and our value to him. The inner work that the Holy Spirit does in our lives is further evidence of God's recreation mandate for us. We often think of our salvation as a momentary act, but the Spirit's work in us is ongoing, and certainly developing the fruits of the Spirit[151] is a lifetime's calling. This shows God's ongoing commitment to us, expressed through the idea of the Spirit being the 'paraclete', the one who comes alongside.

So, in a very real sense Jesus continues to empathise with us as he indwells us by his Spirit. This becomes his ongoing work rather than just a one-off encounter with humanity limited to his thirty-three years of life in human form. The Holy Spirit in us both connects us to the Godhead but also connects the Godhead to us in a very tangible way, not to mention the fact that as we share this one Holy Spirit we are connected to each other as members of his body: 'For we were all baptised by one Spirit so as to form one body – whether Jews or Gentiles, slave or free – and we were all given the one Spirit to drink.'[152]

---

151. Galatians 5:22-23.
152. 1 Corinthians 12:13.

Another dimension to look at here is the fact that Jesus carries the scars of his earthly life in his resurrected body. I was running a session on 'the gospel and shame' at one church when the vicar, as part of our discussion time, highlighted that Jesus' resurrected body carried his earthly scars, which got me thinking.

We know his scars still showed because of his resurrection appearance to Thomas where he shows him the wounds from the cross as part of the proof of who he is. 'Then he said to Thomas, "Put your finger here; see my hands. Reach out your hand and put it into my side. Stop doubting and believe."'[153] In this way, Jesus carries into the heavenly places the marks of his life of empathy with us. What a remarkable connection; earth and heaven are joined through the suffering demonstrated in the reality of these scars.

One of the results of our shame culture seems to be the rise in self-harming. The statistics are rising, especially among younger people.[154] The wounds thus inflicted and the scars that remain, like Jesus' scars, will be carried by those who harm themselves in this way. I think it is a beautiful insight here to have these scars visible in Jesus' resurrected body as proof of his humanity carried into his resurrected body; not a dismissing of his earthly experience, but a recognition of its reality and pain. In this way, once again we connect the reality of our lives with our future hope.

One couple spoke to me on the door as they were leaving our meeting one Sunday. They wanted to talk to me about the communion we had taken during the service that morning. They had a more traditional church background and were enjoying the different approach that we were taking but often had questions, which I always welcomed.

---

153. John 20:27.
154. Rohan Borschmann, Stuart A. Kinner, 'Responding to the rising prevalence of self-harm', *The Lancet*, 4 June 2019. https://www.thelancet.com/journals/lanpsy/article/PIIS2215-0366(19)30210-X/fulltext (accessed 11.10.21).

The question on this occasion was simple; they asked if I could lead the communion in a more traditional way and in particular asked, could I use the set words from the Anglican Holy Communion service? I found myself being surprisingly firm with them that I didn't necessarily think that would be a good idea. This surprised them, as I am usually quite open to including people's suggestions. I realised they had touched a nerve in me and were getting an unexpected response because of this.

My memory of the more traditional liturgy used around the communion service was of a focus on us being sinners rather than saints; coming in need of forgiveness, being unworthy to receive from God etc etc. I told them the way I wanted to approach communion was more around who we have now become and what Jesus has made possible for us. In other words, to look at and celebrate the new covenant.

My response was out of proportion to the simple question they had asked, and I realised that I had intuitively moved away from the place of seeing us as sinners and moved to a place where I wanted to celebrate and remember that we are saints.

Chapter 18: Is Honour Relevant in Our Context?

Jesus now receives glory at the Father's right hand and is honoured by him

> Therefore God exalted him to the highest place and gave him the name that is above every name, that at the name of Jesus every knee should bow, in heaven and on earth and under the earth, and every tongue acknowledge that Jesus Christ is Lord, to the glory of God the Father.[155]

Earlier we looked at how Jesus received honour from his Father whilst here on earth. He is also honoured as he ascends to re-join the Trinity.

The idea of honour is very much part of the undoing of shame in a cultural sense.

> Ruth Benedict argues that Japanese culture is shaped primarily by an extreme awareness to social hierarchy, honor, virtue and duty (on and giri). These social patterns, play out in every social action, from war to child-rearing. Benedict states that '"On" not only means obligation, but also debt, loyalty, kindness and love, and debt in Japan has to be carried the best an individual can' (Benedict, 1946). The word on doesn't have a proper explanation since the English word obligation doesn't contain all the meanings of on. Benedict explains the attitude about indebtedness by giving an example of a word that Japanese use and is stronger than thank you. That word is katajikenai, and it is written with the Kanjis 'insult,' 'loss of face'.[156]

---

155. Philippians 2:9-11.
156. Japan info, *The Chrysanthemum and the Sword*, short review (8 June 2015), https://jpninfo.com/10394 (accessed 8.12.20). Ruth Benedict, *The Chrysanthemum and the Sword* (Boston, MA: Houghton Mifflin, 1946).

As I have reflected on this area I have come to see that what we are experiencing in our Western world as it relates to shame is somewhat different from the cultural shame of more traditional shame cultures. The outward constructs that shape the shame environment and cause a 'loss of face' are not there in quite the same way. I think this is partly due to the extreme individualisation of our Western culture. So the shame experienced in our culture, whilst it has a collective component, is more focused around individual relationships and in my observation is driven by envy on a personal level rather than loss of face in a more communal setting. This is highlighted through Lucy's story that we looked at earlier.

An example of this would be where we are seen to be 'living the life'. Posting our highlights on social media and downplaying what life is like in reality for us. This competitive one-upmanship creates hierarchy in which we try to outdo others so we can have the place of honour. Or, to put it another way, we might choose not to post something for fear of looking inferior. Our popularity is measured in the number of 'likes' or the number of followers we have.

So, it is in this different setting that we need to consider how the idea of honour is played out and has relevance. Whilst it has a part to play in more traditional shame cultures, what part might honour have to play, if any, in our current situation? This is the work of contextualisation, looking at how metaphors connect with current experience and so resonate in a way that makes sense and is helpful.

Let's start that journey as we look at this word 'honour'. To honour' means to hold someone in high esteem or with great respect; to honour someone can also mean to admire and look up to them. These were all true in my earlier story about my woodwork teacher. He was highly skilled as a woodworker, and had a position of authority in the school as a teacher. To honour can also be used in reference to keeping an agreement.

Whilst the word itself works in more traditional cultures, it does not resonate with ours in quite the same way. We therefore need to see what does, and how we can explain what that might mean in terms of the gospel and how it relates to Jesus being honoured and accepted back into relationship with God the Father.

If we go back to basics and take one definition of shame as being 'there is something wrong with me' then the opposite of that would be to say there is 'something right with me' or 'I am all right'. The challenge here is to see this in terms of personhood linked to and driven by identity, rather than being seen to 'do the right thing' and as a result to be 'all right'.

This is where empathy comes alive, because it steps right into the place where you find yourself, even though your actions are not attractive or inviting. In that sense, it is sacrificial and looks beyond what is being displayed; it sees something of value behind the outward actions and steps towards that rather than being pushed away by the unhelpful actions. So we hold each person in high esteem, and step towards them with integrity, in this way we show honour.

I have spent many hours in conversation with a good friend, David, about the topic of shame. He works as a psychologist helping those with eating disorders and so is very familiar with this area of shame, as it is central to his work. During one of our conversations, David suggested I looked at the place of righteousness and how it connects with shame to see if it might be better in our setting than honour. Again, righteousness is not so much in current parlance but it does have obvious biblical overtones. I turned to the dictionary once again here, this time to D.B. Garlington and the *New Dictionary of Christian Ethics and Pastoral Theology*, which was particularly illuminating from a biblical perspective:

The Biblical idea of righteousness is rooted in creation. In Eden a family bond (or covenant) was established. Genesis 1 and 2 record God's pledge to bless, multiply and sustain the human beings made to hold fellowship with him and be the recipient of his fatherly care. It is loyalty to this relationship of mutual love and faithfulness which is called 'righteousness'.[157]

So we see the biblical understanding of this word has strong relational roots – to be in right relationship with God is at the heart of its meaning. This relationship 'of mutual love', as Garlington describes it, is what is called righteousness. So we could say to 'be all right' in biblical terms, to be righteous, is to have our being substantiated in and through our relationship with God.

This is an alternative to the use of the word 'honour', which as I said earlier is often used in the context of cultural shame but does not resonate in the same way in our Western cultural view. Righteousness conveys the idea of right standing in the same way that honour does, but is less helpful in that it implies a view that we have gained that right standing through 'right actions' rather than finding it through relationship, which is the biblical basis. More work is needed here to find words that work in our current context. We need to listen out for the language that is in use and use it where applicable, but also look to those more qualified in this area to help us develop language that connects well.

He has opened up the way for us to be part of God's family

The banishment that was the result of Adam and Eve choosing their independence from God in Genesis 3:23 meant that God would no longer walk with them 'in the garden in the cool of the day'. This

---

157. D.B. Garlington, *New Dictionary of Christian Ethics and Pastoral Theology* (Leicester: IVP, 1995), p. 743.

banishment has been overturned by Jesus and we are welcomed back into relationship with the Trinity, introduced to God the Father by the Son, with whom we are joint heirs, as the Holy Spirit resides in us as a 'guarantee of our inheritance'.[158]

> For those who are led by the Spirit of God are the children of God. The Spirit you received does not make you slaves, so that you live in fear again; rather, the Spirit you received brought about your adoption to sonship. And by him we cry, '*Abba*, Father.' The Spirit himself testifies with our spirit that we are God's children. Now if we are children, then we are heirs – heirs of God and co-heirs with Christ, if indeed we share in his sufferings in order that we may also share in his glory.[159]

Our adoption as sons and daughters is ultimately what overcomes our feelings of shame. As shame is about a loss of identity, this leads to feelings of inadequacy, rejection and isolation, and the fact that God adopts us as children is indeed good news to this situation. Our identity is restored as we see God as our father, Jesus as our brother, and the Holy Spirit dwelling in us, empowering us to live out our new life.

This relational context takes things out of the more binary approach that is sometimes taken to our salvation where it is often seen as an exchange mechanism. What this shift to the relational does is to open up the thinking space in which we understand our salvation and creates a more complex and sometimes messy relational setting for us. Here is one such example from Galatians 4, which takes some grappling with. Notice how a number of the factors we have been looking at come together in these verses:

> What I am saying is that as long as an heir is underage, he is no different from a slave, although he owns the whole estate. The

---

158. Ephesians 1:14, ESV.
159. Romans 8:14-17.

heir is subject to guardians and trustees until the time set by his father. So also, when we were under age, we were in slavery under the elemental spiritual forces of the world. But when the set time had fully come, God sent his Son, born of a woman, born under the law, to redeem those under the law, that we might receive adoption to son-ship. Because you are his sons, God sent the Spirit of his Son into our hearts, the Spirit who calls out, '*Abba, Father.*' So you are no longer a slave, but God's child; and since you are his child, God has made you also an heir.[160]

It is interesting to see how the law is used in this context. We are living under the law because we are underage and so we are subject to our guardians. In this way, although we own the estate, we operate in the same manor as slaves because we are subject to our guardians in the same way that slaves are subject to their masters. In this underage state, we are in slavery to the 'elemental spiritual forces of the world'. Notice what happens to free us from this slavery. Just as a child comes of age at the time appointed by his father, so we come of age and take our inheritance as we become sons and daughters of God.

In this way, we move from being slaves under the law to our guardians, and become adopted children of God. This happens in a rather fascinating way. God the Father becomes the father who sets the time that we will come of age; that time comes as Jesus is born, 'born of a woman ... under the law'. Notice the empathy connection: Jesus comes into the space we occupy, 'born of a woman ... under the law' to redeem us. We are all potential heirs, we are 'image bearers', but we can only come of age and become full heirs when we are redeemed by Jesus. We then have the Spirit of the Son living in our hearts.

Our identity is not now determined by being 'under the elemental spiritual forces of the world' but is instead grounded in the fact that we

---

160. Galatians 4:1-7.

are God's children and have his Spirit living in us. This moves us from 'positional' identity to 'relational' identity. By this I mean that under the law we are compared to slaves, which gives us a positional identity within the structure of the culture. As we are redeemed from this, we move to a relational identification as sons.

As I mentioned earlier, John Zizioulas is particularly helpful in this area as he identifies the difference between personhood and identity. He is the Eastern Orthodox Metropolitan bishop of Pergamon, Greece, and a highly influential theologian noted for building bridges between East and West.

Reflecting on Zizioulas, Eric Hyde highlights the following:

> The contrast of individual and person runs deep in much of Zizioulas' theology. He writes: 'When the Holy Spirit blows, He does not create good individual Christians, individual "saints," but an event of communion, which transforms everything the Spirit touches in to a *relational being.*' When God creates, He creates in His own image – He creates 'persons.'[161]

The idea of personhood is intrinsically linked to relationship. We are who we are because of those around us. We become fully who we were created to be as we live in relationship with others. Our identity is completely linked to these relationships as we are created in God's image who is in himself in relationship as Father, Son and Holy Spirit.

> In other words, the Persons of the Trinity are Persons precisely because they are in communion with one another.[162]

Our highly individualistic culture in the West tends to overlook this

161. Eric Hyde, 'The Individual and the Church: John Zizioulas and the Eastern Orthodox Perspective', 27 December 2011, https://ehyde.wordpress.com/2011/12/27/the-individual-and-the-church-john-zizioulas-and-the-eastern-orthodox-perspective (accessed 8.12.20).
162. Ibid.

relational dimension and we have been caught up in this as Christians as well, focusing on the life of the individual at the expense of seeing personhood as fully understood and developed in the context of relationship.

The gospel as described from the guilt perspective tends to deal with substance in isolation based often in abstract concepts. As we look at a gospel that connects with shame, we shift from this individualistic view which, as I mentioned earlier, makes it somewhat transactional, to a more relational context which shame operates in.

So, our identity is determined by our personhood, which is founded and formed from our relationships. In this way, what happens when we become children of God is that our personhood is defined through our relationship to the Godhead. This is enabled in a Trinitarian fashion as we see in the verses above from Galatians. The Father sets the timing, 'when the set time had fully come, God sent his Son'. The Son brings redemption by coming amongst us, 'born under the law, to redeem those under the law'. Then the Spirit comes into our hearts 'God sent the Spirit of his Son into our hearts'.[163] This three-fold participation in creating our new personhood will be a necessary part of our gospel telling by emphasising the relational components involved.

I am indebted to my friend Jeremy Follett who introduced me to Zizioulas' writing and encouraged me in my own research as he himself carried out further studies on leadership in the Church of England.

---

163. Galatians 4:4-6.

Chapter 19: Raised Up With Christ

Taking our place with Jesus as a new creation

> And God raised us up with Christ and seated us with him in the heavenly realms in Christ Jesus, in order that in the coming ages he might show the incomparable riches of his grace, expressed in his kindness to us in Christ Jesus. For it is by grace you have been saved, through faith – and this is not from yourselves, it is the gift of God – not by works, so that no one can boast. For we are God's handiwork, created in Christ Jesus to do good works, which God prepared in advance for us to do.[164]

> Since, then, you have been raised with Christ, set your hearts on things above, where Christ is, seated at the right hand of God. Set your minds on things above, not on earthly things. For you died, and your life is now hidden with Christ in God.[165]

God raises us up with Christ; he sees us as saints, not sinners!

We are indeed new creations as we live as those whose life is 'now hidden with Christ in God'. This changes the way we think about ourselves – yes, we need to die to ourselves daily, but we are raised to live life in all its fullness in Christ. We can live as children of the light[166] as we live this side of the resurrection. We don't have to live under the shadow of the cross in a way that keeps us constantly reminded of our sinful nature.

We often think of these verses in the future tense, i.e. linked to the idea that we will be raised up at the resurrection of the dead, because

---

164. Ephesians 2:6-10.
165. Colossians 3:1-3.
166. John 12:36.

we have our 'ticket to heaven'. However, this is not just a future reality, but rather a current one. 'You have been raised with Christ': this has happened and we are called to live in this reality by '[setting our] minds on things above'.

It may be worth pausing for a moment and asking what the dominant themes are in the Christian communities we are a part of; where does the focus tend to go? The ways we relate together, the language we use, and in particular the liturgy and words that are formalised in our practices, these all have a part to play in establishing the culture of our Christian communities. I wonder how much of what we do and, in particular, what we say creates a sense of shame that is unhelpful for people?

In a recent paper on shame, Andrea Campanale picks up this issue. I have include her full written liturgy here with her permission as an example of contextualisation when it comes to the words we might use in our Christian communities:

Currently much of what we say in church actually reinforces shame. Confession compounds shame and our liturgy assumes pride rather than a crippling sense of unworthiness and the desire to hide our true selves. I have therefore begun to write and use others' 'shame-free' liturgies in our worship. Here is an example of a Eucharistic prayer that I have written. I hope it is relevant to the issue and does not induce shame in those who are reciting it:

Screen Eucharist
The Lord is here
Our TV dinner is served

Lift up your hearts
Shielded to hide the wounds and scars

Let us give thanks to the Lord our God

Because you have sufficiently engaged our interest for the time being

We sit before you, side by side, isolated and distant.

Hoping to be distracted, entertained, transported to an alternative existence.

We eat without tasting, we gather without noticing, locked in a conversation that takes place between our ears.

Yet the God-man Jesus invites us to dine with Him tonight.

A table has been laid and He waits for us to take our place beside Him.

A banquet has been prepared and our favourite dishes are set before us.

He wants to know us. He is curious about our thoughts, preferences and dreams.

For through Him all experience of life, love and the created world was made possible.

We are a reflection of His goodness and embodied potential for newness.

We are so grateful that because He practised what He preached to the point of dying to maintain His authenticity, we don't have to live up to the expectations of our ideal self.

We can be free to reveal who we really are and find that we are worthy to be loved by God and those with whom we long to be in relationship.

Even death on a cross could not stop Him fulfilling his purpose and He rose to a new life.

We thank you that this means we too can look forward to our pain and loss being transformed into faith and hope if we choose to trust Him in vulnerability.

Jesus returned to Heaven so He could advocate on our behalf but He sent us a helper, the Holy Spirit, who gives us divinely inspired visions and insights to encourage and direct us.

Because of all that has been done for us in Jesus Christ, we can join with angels and all those who have gone before, praising God and saying:

Holy, holy, holy Lord
God of provision and presence
heaven and earth are full of your glory
Hosanna in the highest

Blessed is the one who comes in the name of the Lord.
Hosanna in the highest.

May we live an integrated life where we are at one with ourselves and actively looking to make the most of every opportunity to partner with you in bringing peace, healing and justice to the spheres where we have influence, as Christ demonstrated for us.

Who in the same night that he was betrayed with a kiss,
took bread, gave thanks, broke it and shared it amongst his friends, saying,

'Take, eat; this is my body which is given for you;

do this in remembrance of me.'

In the same way, after supper he took a cup and gave you thanks:

he gave it to them, saying,

'Drink this, all of you;

this is my blood which marks a new relationship between humanity and the divine,

it removes all fears, regrets and hurts you have inflicted on yourselves and others, that has kept us from one another.

Do this, as often as you drink it,

in remembrance of me.

Christ has died

Christ is risen

Christ will come again

So as we remember the freedom and healing Christ offers us, we look forward to a day when He will return and restore all creation to beauty and wholeness.

Until then turn us from the impassive screen to see your reflected glory in the eyes of those we keep at arm's length.

Help us risk intimacy and build community such that the value of relationship is displayed and we show how dreams of a better and fairer world become reality when we live and work together in unity, diversity and mutuality.

We invite your Holy Spirit so this bread might become your body which sustains us and the wine your blood that reconciles us.

Empower and motivate us with your love.

Give us the strength to bear our suffering and disappointment.

Keep us discontent with living vicariously through the shallow and distorted image of 'the good life' as portrayed by celebrities.

And we look forward to coming home, where we are safe and loved, honest and fulfilled.

For it is only through our loving Creator, redeeming Son and enabling Spirit we can be assured that one day our longing will cease and all we have desired and glimpsed will be known in full.

Amen

This is just one attempt at shame-free liturgy and I think there is much to do in creating resources that take the problem of shame seriously and help facilitate reconciliation with God and one another while remaining faithful to the tradition.[167] </q>

As I read Andrea's words I am reminded of Paul's words from Colossians; 'So then, just as you received Christ Jesus as Lord, continue to live your

---

167. Eds Jonny Baker and Cathy Ross, *The Pioneer Gift* (Norwich: Canterbury Press, 2014), pp. 191-194.

lives in him, rooted and built up in him, strengthened in the faith as you were taught, and overflowing with thankfulness.'[168] So, whether the words we use are set liturgy as written above, or even if we come from a more extemporised tradition, it is well worth looking at the diet of language we use and the emphasis it has. A good way to do this in less formal settings is to listen to the language people use when they pray. What are their assumptions about where they are in their relationship with God; how do they see themselves and others? It goes without saying that listening to ourselves and the language we use as we pray is also very insightful and revealing.

---

168. Colossians 2:6-7.

Chapter 20: The Spirit of God Lives in You

God shows his acceptance of us as sons and daughters by sending his Holy Spirit to live in us

> You, however, are not in the realm of the flesh but are in the realm of the Spirit, if indeed the Spirit of God lives in you. And if anyone does not have the Spirit of Christ, they do not belong to Christ. But if Christ is in you, then even though your body is subject to death because of sin, the Spirit gives life because of righteousness. And if the Spirit of him who raised Jesus from the dead is living in you, he who raised Christ from the dead will also give life to your mortal bodies because of his Spirit who lives in you.[169]

This is indeed an amazing concept – that God chooses to come and inhabit us with His Holy Spirit.

As far as shame is concerned, this gives us not only a sense of being valued by God, but also connection to Him and a deep sense of ownership by Him.

'The Spirit of God lives in you'; this is the Spirit that cries out *'Abba, Father,*[170] the Spirit that confirms our identity as sons and daughters of God; without this indwelling Spirit we have no confirmation of our family likeness. It is through the Spirit's indwelling that we become like God as he takes up his dwelling in us. We have our identity restored. Jesus talks to the disciples about this at length as part of his farewell discourse in John 14:

> And I will ask the Father, and he will give you another advocate to help you and be with you for ever – the Spirit of truth. The world

---

169. Romans 8:9-11.
170. Galatians 4:6.

cannot accept him, because it neither sees him nor knows him. But you know him, for he lives with you and will be in you. I will not leave you as orphans; I will come to you.[171]

So, we are no longer orphans. Those who live with shame often live with this sense of abandonment and an unsettled sense of being rejected, or fear that they will be rejected by others. Knowing that we are not orphaned and that God has not abandoned us will be a key area in this respect. We can become highly sensitised to any hint of rejection or being misunderstood and therefore disconnected.

Jesus' language here is paramount in addressing this feeling of abandonment: his affirmation of the Father's love and the beautiful phrase that 'we will come ... and make our home with them' is overwhelming and such a good metaphor for those dealing with shame. Making a home together, a place of belonging, acceptance and inclusion: 'Anyone who loves me will obey my teaching. My Father will love them, and we will come to them and make our home with them.'[172]

We have echoes here of the relationship in the garden, with God walking 'in the cool of the day',[173] and the restoration of relationship once lost – now restored as God comes and make his home once again, not just walking beside us but by indwelling us.

I discovered a fascinating insight a few years ago. The original phrase 'to be made in his image' from Genesis 1:27 has as its root the idea of 'indwelling' and it was also the word used for an Idol in the surrounding cultures. This may sound a bit strange, except when you understand that these other cultures believed that their gods came and inhabited their idols. This, then, sets the stage for our understanding of what has been lost, namely the indwelling presence of God. So as we receive the Spirit given by Jesus, our original design is restored.

171. John 14:16-18.
172. John 14:23.
173. Genesis 3:8.

'Before long, the world will not see me any more, but you will see me. Because I live, you also will live. On that day you will realise that I am in my Father, and you are in me, and I am in you.'[174] It is easy to put this verse in the context of Jesus' second coming; however, the reference to 'On that day' is not about the distant future, but the more immediate one when the Holy Spirit will be sent. By his indwelling we will be in Jesus and he will be in us, just as he is in the Father. In this way because he lives we also will live; this is a 'here and now' statement about us being fully alive as God intended from the beginning with his indwelling.

So there is a sense in which Adam and Eve throw away who they truly are as they listen to the voice of the serpent. They look for an independent identity and in doing this they lose their true identity in God. Just as God says, in Genesis 2:17, by doing this they die. So their sin is two-fold: it is a rejection of God and a devaluing of who they truly are.

We live with this sense of denial of who we really are; it resonates with us and in particular this generation. There is a sense of loss around who we could be or may have been. This does not have to be the case; we can find our true identity and sense of value as we explore our true personhood as those created by God in his image, having his Spirit indwelling us as it was always meant to be.

---

174. John 14:19-20.

Chapter 21: New Life Offered as Part of a New Community Here on Earth

So in Christ we, though many, form one body, and each member belongs to all the others.[175]

For we were all baptised by one Spirit so as to form one body – whether Jews or Gentiles, slave or free – and we were all given the one Spirit to drink.[176]

With all that we have said about relationship being key to the restoration of personhood, and having dipped into how this relates to our relationship with God, we also need to consider the role that our Christian communities play in this respect.

Again, because of our cultural focus on individual salvation often at the expense of the larger relational context, we may have overlooked some important dynamics here. We are saved into a relationship with God on a vertical axis, if you like, but also into a relationship with our brothers and sisters in the Christian community, both local and global. These relationships with each other bring a horizontal dimension to our salvation. I regularly have conversations with people who tell me they are Christians but practise their faith on their own and don't connect with other Christians. Their faith is purely a private matter between them and God. We need to challenge this idea with its focus totally on the vertical dimension and individual setting of our faith. We need to be reminded that as the Holy Spirit works in us, his creative work is always in the context of relationship. Our conversion through recreation is always into 'persons'. In this way, the creation he performs as we are

---

175. Romans 12:5.
176. 1 Corinthians 12:13.

redeemed is 'in his own image'[177] – a central part of our redemption is into relationship; into the body of Christ, into communion with God and his people.

The need of a shame-carrying person (which incidentally is true of all of us, but more evident in some than others) to be included and to feel that they are accepted and belong is really strong, and so this acceptance and belonging will need to be a major consideration in our gospel message for the shame context. So many of Jesus' stories are about this: two obvious ones would have to be the parable of the great banquet in Luke 14 and, of course, in Luke 15 the story of the lost son – the two shameful sons find reconciliation and welcome from their father. This is a picture of Jesus' radical table fellowship with shamed sinners.

Telling the stories is one thing, creating Christian communities that offer welcome and acceptance in the way that the stories portray is, however, quite another!

Zizioulas writes:

> There is a pathology built into the very roots of our existence, inherited through our birth, and that is the fear of the other. This is a result of the rejection of the Other par excellence, our Creator, by the first Man, Adam ... The essence of sin is the fear of the Other, which is part of this rejection. Once the affirmation of the 'self' is realized through the rejection and not the acceptance of the Other ... it is only natural and inevitable for the other to become an enemy and a threat.[178]

I have seen this fear exhibited by others and indeed myself on numerous occasions. I sense it in myself and have to combat it regularly. I wonder how often the 'affirmation of the "self"' is realized through the rejection

---

177. Genesis 1:27.
178. John D. Zizioulas, *Communion and Otherness* (Edinburgh: T&T Clark, 2006), pp. 1-2.

and not the acceptance of the Other'? You may like to pause for a moment and consider how this works for you.

This concept of sin, whilst linked to the wrongdoing idea that creates the guilt concept is, in my view, deeper than that. This is because it has at its root the drive of the ego to put our self as an individual in a place of superiority by rejecting the other person. In this way, we find our sense of identity at the expense of another rather than in relationship and through the enhancement of the other person.

Where wrongdoing is our basis for needing salvation, then judgement of that wrongdoing becomes paramount. This very easily tips over into a judgement not just of the wrongdoing but also of the person carrying it out. The two can become inextricably linked. This further compounds the threat of the other person, who is not like us.

However, when shame and loss of relationship is the basis for needing salvation, then the acceptance of the other becomes paramount and an integral part of the salvation act. This poses a heap of challenges for us to work through. Not least of which is that we will be sceptical in the West of the suggestion that we as Christian communities have a role to play in bringing about salvation – that somehow we are an integral part of God's act of salvation. This will take a shift in our mindset. It is part of the move from an individual concept of salvation to a more communal one.

As the language used for the Church is 'the body of Christ' (1 Corinthians 12:27), it should come as no surprise that our personhood both as individuals and as a community now becomes associated with his (Jesus), because we are part of that body, and not only his, but also the Father and the Spirit because they are inextricably linked through their relationships.

This more communal and relational way of seeing things needs to permeate our way of thinking. As we adopt these ideas we will have to re-evaluate some of our institutional constructs which have not always served a more relational way of operating.

One idea that has helped me consider this shift is that of the 'bounded set' versus the 'centred set'. This idea was published by Dr Paul G. Hiebert in an article called 'Conversion, Culture, and Cognitive Categories'[179]

I first came across this idea several years ago and found it really helpful as we worked out how we would shape our community in the church I help to lead. In essence, a 'Bounded Set' is just as it says, really – a group formed around common characteristics that define them as individuals. To be part of the group you have to be within the boundary of these characteristics.

So, as a teenager I was encouraged to get baptised so that I could become a member of the Baptist church that I was attending. In getting baptised I was crossing the boundary from being 'out' to being 'in'. So, a common characteristic in this situation was that those who were in the bounded set had been baptised. This gave me the privilege of having 'say so' by voting at the church meeting.

In this way, it was easy to define who was in and who was out and the mission of the church was clear: to get more people in, to get them across the line of membership through baptism and the other procedures that followed. This caused me some discomfort as I was reluctant to work with such clear-cut boundaries that made judgements about who was in and who was out. It didn't seem to take into account the softer factors involved and the differences in people's approach to faith.

It came as something of a relief to find there was another way of looking at this, which thought about the idea of a boundary in a totally different way. Hiebert calls this the 'Centered Set' idea. It works as the name suggests on the concept that there is a centre that you are either

179. Dr Paul G. Hiebert, 'Conversion, Culture, and Cognitive Categories', *Gospel in Context* 1 (4), 1978, pp. 24-29, https://danutm.files.wordpress.com/2010/06/hiebert-paul-g-conversion-culture-and-cognitive-categories.pdf (accessed 8.12.20).

moving towards or away from. The set is defined as those who are moving towards the centre point.

This makes it more dynamic and allows for fluidity; it also takes pace into account, as some will be moving slower than others, but still heading towards the centre. It allows for the centre to be defined in more relational terms and gives greater scope for relational understanding as a result. It also allows for a greater variety of contribution because you are not categorising people around a clear-cut boundary and trying to create conformity, but happy to work more openly with diversity and instead encourage a direction of travel.

Hiebert summarises it helpfully this way:

A centered set approach to defining 'Christian' corresponds more closely to what we see happening in mission and church growth. It also seems to correspond more closely with the Hebraic view of reality.

But a centred set approach does raise some problems, at least for Westerners who think primarily in terms of bounded sets. These problems often relate to the question, how do you organize an institution such as the church as a centered set? Is it not essential to maintain the boundaries by setting high standards for membership?

On the other hand, the bounded set fits best with our Western view of the world and our democratic ways of organizing associations such as the church. Ultimately the question of whether we should see the term 'Christian' as a bounded or as a centered set must be decided on theological, not pragmatic principles. But this demands that we think through all of the basic theological terms and decide which of these should be viewed as bounded sets, and which as centred sets.[180]

---

180. Ibid.

Finding ways of including people rather than excluding them will be part of our challenge as we work to see the gospel connect with shame. I think it is essential that we look at how our organisations work in terms of who belongs and how they get to belong. The centred set idea opens up some new possibilities in this respect and gives us a different way to have conversations about this vital issue. It goes without saying that the person at the centre that we are moving towards is Jesus; but even here we need to be open to seeing this in a more relational and community sense, rather than from our Western individualistic perspective.

Commenting on Zizioulas, Hyde writes:

Christ Himself becomes revealed as truth not 'in' a community, but 'as' a community. So truth is not just something 'expressed' or 'heard;' a propositional or logical truth; but something which 'is,' i.e. an ontological truth: the community itself becomes the truth.' In this light, it becomes evident why Zizioulas argues for the necessity of the Church for salvation. If the Church truly is the *Body of Christ*, then to be joined with His Body – the community of 'others' – is inherent in being joined to Christ Himself.[181]

Zizioulas lays this out quite clearly and without ambiguity:

In the first place, ecclesial being is bound to the very being of God. From the fact that a human being is a member of the church, he becomes an 'image of God' [sic] he exists as God Himself exists, he takes on Gods [sic] 'way of being.' This way of being is not moral attainment, something that man *accomplishes*. It is a way of relationship with the world, with other people and with God, an

---

181. Eric Hyde, 'The Individual and the Church: John Zizioulas and the Eastern Orthodox Perspective', 27 December 2011, https://ehyde.wordpress.com/2011/12/27/the-individual-and-the-church-john-zizioulas-and-the-eastern-orthodox-perspective/ (accessed 8.12.20).

event of *communion*, and that is why it cannot be realised as the achievement of an *individual*, but only as an *ecclesial* fact.[182]

I have found myself initially reacting quite strongly to these ideas. It faced me up to the reality of how I saw my salvation as a more private and individual relationship with God. Now, I would have always put importance on being a member of the body of Christ – however, I would not have thought of that belonging in the way that Zizioulas expresses it here. So, our redemption is firmly rooted in the relationships of the Christian community; this is not an optional extra as some would like it to be. This means that there is no place for us choosing to be independent Christians doing faith on our own. This 'event of *communion*' as it is so beautifully described here takes on God's 'way of being' living in and through relationship and as such demonstrates our salvation.

In conclusion to Part 2: 'So what?' questions

Through these pages I have just hinted at some of the areas we will want to work with as we think about a gospel message that connects to our shame culture. I am sure there are many more, and even the ones I have highlighted would benefit from greater thought and development. My hope is that this will have whetted your appetite to think and explore further.

Let's take a few moments to reflect on some practical points that come out of what we have looked at so far. Or, to put it another way, let's ask the 'So what?' questions. Here are a few questions, which may stimulate some reflection for you.

1) How does this perspective shape our mission mandate?

2) The tone of voice we use?

---

182. John D. Zizioulas, *Being as Communion* (Darton, Longman & Todd, 2004), p. 15.

3) Implications for one to one conversations?

4) Implications for group discussion?

5) Implications for our Christian communities and what they look like?

6) Implications for our outreach as Christian communities?

Part 3
Implications for Our Christian Communities

Introduction to Part 3

We are now shifting in emphasis as we enter this last section so I have taken time to explain this here. In this third section I want to move us from thinking about the gospel message and how we might share it with others, to thinking about our Christian communities and what they may need to look like in light of how we are now thinking about the gospel.

I think this is essential, as these two areas need to connect and validate each other. If this is not the case, we will be saying one thing and living another. Stuart Murray Williams emphasises this as he writes:

> Neglecting the health and inner life of missional communities undermines the confidence of those who are sharing faith with their friends, disenchants any who begin to belong before they believe and accelerates the exodus of leavers. Building healthy, honest and harmonious communities is a prerequisite for effective mission.[183]

The words of James come to mind here:

> Do not merely listen to the word, and so deceive yourselves. Do what it says. Anyone who listens to the word but does not do what it says is like someone who looks at his face in a mirror and, after looking at himself, goes away and immediately forgets what he looks like. But whoever looks intently into the perfect law that gives freedom and continues in it – not forgetting what they have heard but doing it – they will be blessed in what they do.[184]

---

183. Stuart Murray, *Church After Christendom* (Milton Keynes: Paternoster Press, 2004), p. 165.
184. James 1:22-25.

Each year I have the privilege of leading the local schools' work team called Step, which I mentioned earlier, on a reflection day as they start the new academic year. We review the year just gone and think together about what is coming in the New Year ahead. As part of 2018's reflection day, we revisited the previous year's thoughts around how the gospel message needed to be reshaped to connect with this younger generation. We looked together at the shift from guilt to shame and some of the areas we have explored in the opening section of this book. The schools' work team were, as ever, ahead of the game with this, as it has become day-to-day thinking for them as they engaged with teenagers in schools. Once you see the difference, it pops up everywhere.

I liken it to getting a new car. We had a very faithful Toyota Previa as our children were growing up. It was ideally suited to us as it transported the six of us and still had room for friends. They were quite a common site and we would point them out as we drove around. Times change, however, and the children have grown up and the Toyota was not needed any more, so after some eighteen years of faithful service it has been replaced by an equally functional but, as I thought, less popular Citroën Berlingo. This is basically a van with seats in the back – very uncool; my daughter vowed she would not come in the car with me if I got one! I have, however, won her over, as it has proved invaluable to take her and all her belongings to university! I never really saw any of these when we had the Toyota, but now, of course, I see them everywhere. So it is with the shame idea, somehow when you become aware of it and start to see what it looks like, you bump into it all over the place. This is what started to happen to the schools' work team over several years. So much so that they became aware of the gap between what they were thinking about in school and how out of sync this felt with the local churches they attended who were still largely working with the guilt language and concepts.

The Christian communities that we create need to resonate with the life-giving message of the gospel. Particularly in our current context, this life-giving message needs to demonstrate how it relates to our release from the captivity of shame. This could have some challenging consequences for the way we think about how we meet together and how we relate to each other in our Christian communities.

I guess an obvious opener might be to simply take Brené Brown's three things that shame thrives on, namely 'secrecy, silence and judgement' and according to her research, what enables shame to grow exponentially. What would it look like to see the opposite of these three things outworked in our communities? Instead of secrecy, we will endeavour to be open and transparent. Instead of silence, we will endeavour to give each other a voice and the honour of being listened to. Then thirdly, we will offer communities that are not bringing judgement.

Before we rush headlong into what all that might mean, I want us to spend some time taking a larger overview so let's step back for a moment. I have found Jayson Georges' book *The 3D Gospel* very helpful and used it a great deal. I have both taught and reflected on how our culture has changed and what that means for us in terms of our witness in both word and deed. Georges outlines three culture stereotypes that in his view the message of gospel needs to connect with. These are guilt and innocence, fear and power and shame and honour.

In summary he suggests that the guilt-focused cultures mainly found in the West are individualistic in nature, they use a metaphor of the court room when it comes to the gospel, and tend to be historically Christian. As we have already said, this has given a focus on wrongdoing and the question being asked here is: how can my sins be forgiven?

Georges' ideas around Fear and Power are taken from the more African worldview; this he sees played out through a metaphor of combat and takes on a military air as evil in the form of the devil is fought. The question in this context becomes: how can I access the power to control my life?

The third view that is highlighted is Shame and Honour. This is seen as predominantly Eastern, although it has become prominent in the West in recent times. 'The metaphor is community (relational) and the resulting question is: how can I be part of the community and be respected?'[185]

Our dominant Western culture, Jayson suggests, is based on the Guilt and Innocence idea. I think we can see how our Christian communities have both imbibed and sought to reach this culture and in doing so emphasised the fact that we are guilty and need forgiveness. The legal metaphor means that we tend to see things in a transactional sense often leading to a need to get things right and a focus on task over relationship. This has shaped our Christian faith in a very particular way and a bit like the goldfish who is unaware of the water it swims in, so we are often unaware of the way our culture has shaped our view of faith and how it works. I have found this to my cost when I have suggested that we could perhaps look at things differently, by proposing that the shame idea may be a better starting place currently!

My hunch is that this historic focus on guilt and innocence and all that spills out from this starting point has had a particular effect on how we see the Church and what it is trying to achieve. This can be seen in how the Church is organised, how it is led and who leads it, who can be part of it and how they join etc. This is to be expected, as our Christian communities exist in the culture and are influenced and affected by it. Our hope is, of course, that the reverse is also true, in that we bring a kingdom influence that spills out of our Christian communities and influences the existing culture that we live in.

---

185. Jayson Georges, 'Theology Guide', *The 3D Gospel*, http://honorshame.com/wp-content/uploads/2014/10/Theology-Guide-Guilt-Shame-Fear-Georges.pdf (accessed 8.12.20). More fully expounded in *The 3D Gospel: Ministry in Guilt, Shame, and Fear Cultures.*

From our historic guilt and innocence starting point, many of the things we do are understood in transactional terms, played out in an emphasis on roles and who does what. We tend to work on a contractual basis, which is built on an exchange mechanism. I will do this, and in return will receive something back. A contract can be either written or verbal and allows an agreement to be enforceable by law. We are familiar with contracts of employment or rental.

This feels just, and stops either party feeling guilty. So we join a Christian community and if it doesn't give us what we are looking for, then we feel completely justified in leaving and will go and join another one to see if that has better things to offer us or our families. This contractual idea underpins a lot of the way we think and work. This is at odds, I would suggest, with our view of God and the heart of the Christian faith. The God we believe in is not a contractual God, he works on the idea of covenant. This gives a different basis for the way he encourages us to operate, setting the parameters in a more relational context which is different from that of contracts.

In his book *Jesus the Saviour*, Marshall outlines the differences well when he writes:

> In modern times we define a host of relations by contracts. These are usually for goods or services and for hard cash. The contract, formal or informal, helps to specify failure in these relationships. The Lord did not establish a contract with Israel or with the church. He created a covenant. There is a difference. Contacts are broken when one of the parties fails to keep his promise. If, let us say, a patient fails to keep an appointment with a doctor, the doctor is not obligated to call the house and inquire, 'Where were you? Why didn't you show up for your appointment?' He simply goes on to his next patient and has his appointment secretary take note of the patient who failed to keep the appointment. The patient may find it harder the next time to see the doctor. He broke an informal contract.

According to the Bible, however, the Lord asks: 'Can a mother forget the baby at her breast and have no compassion on the child she has borne? Though she may forget, I will not forget you!' (Isa. 49:15) The Bible indicates the covenant is more like the ties of a parent to her child than it is a doctor's appointment. If a child fails to show up for dinner, the parent's obligation, unlike the doctor's, isn't cancelled. The parent finds out where the child is and makes sure he's cared for. One member's failure does not destroy the relationship. A covenant puts no conditions on faithfulness. It is the unconditional commitment to love and serve.' – Bruce Shelley[186]

So the biblical idea of covenant sets a very different basis for our relationships together than that of the contract. The transactional dimensions to the contract are well set in our culture and we have to push very hard to work from a different, more covenantal basis.

An example of this would be the way that I have tried to approach building a leadership team at Network (the church that I help to lead). Those who join the central leadership team are not joining to take up roles in the church. They do not have job descriptions that they are expected to carry out. They are there first and foremost as people who will carry leadership. I am asking them to bring themselves primarily, and not just what they can do. This means that they shape the team by being part of it and depending on the particular gifts and personality traits they bring, then the team and the community that we lead together will grow in these areas as well. The covenant idea pushes us back to relationships of trust; these are not defined in the way legal contracts are constructed.

---

186. I.H. Marshall, *Jesus the Savior* (Downers Grove, IL: IVP, 1990), p. 275ff, referenced from Bible.org, https://bible.org/illustration/covenant-not-contract (accessed 8.12.20).

My hope is that this models something of the relationships that we are wanting to develop in and through the community of Network Church. So, our primary reason for being together is not to achieve a particular task, but to bring ourselves and offer them as part of this community. The emphasis is then placed more in who we are than on what we do.

This is further outworked by the fact that this Christian community primarily sees itself as a support for those who are part of it in the roles that they carry beyond it, rather than asking people to join it to carry a role within it. This gives validity to the whole person and includes all that they are and do inside and outside the Christian community that they are part of. Putting the whole person central in this way brings value to them in all that they do and are. This conveyance of value speaks to their personhood and identity not just with words but in the very structure of the way the community works and expresses itself. In this way, it is attempting to value the whole person in all areas of life and wanting to embrace each person and their unique calling to become who God has created them to be in every area of their life.

There obviously needs to be a balance here, as any community needs people to carry roles within it to allow the community to be sustained. However, where the community is built around running programmes, this tends to become the reason the community exists. In this case, the roles needed to support the programmes within it can soon overshadow what the community can offer to help support its members in the roles that they carry outside of it. Conversations with local church leaders regularly highlight this as they struggle to find people, often from their relatively large congregations, to volunteer their services for the various organisations that the church run. This is particularly true in our commuter-belt territory where people work long days and often travel into London on the train.

The other dynamic at play here as seen in *The 3D Gospel* outline above is that the gospel message that has been typically given in our Western culture is one that 'forgives us from our sins and gives us a ticket to heaven'; this is, of course, something of a caricature but in essence probably carries some truth. This plays out in a number of ways when it comes to both the relational dynamics of the Christian communities, as we have been discussing, and the task mandate that it brings.

As part of one Sunday morning looking at *The 3D Gospel* as a way of helping us share our faith in relevant ways, we tipped into a different perspective around these three dimensions to the gospel. As I finished speaking, I opened up the time for feedback and questions which is not uncommon as part of our Sunday teaching time. One of our members was straight up on his feet. I had used three planks to illustrate what I was saying and physically walked along them as I talked about each of the gospel dimensions. In this way, the planks can be seen as bridges that people cross to find faith. It has proven a very helpful way of bringing the idea to life. James was beside me before I could blink and proceeded to walk along each plank in turn. Rather than describe the planks in terms of the words we might use to share what Jesus' death and resurrection were about as I had done, he used them to talk about what church would look like if these planks represented the underlying culture of that particular Christian community. This took us into a completely different but insightful application of these three dimensions. Here is what he highlighted:

> The Shame and Honour plank is empowering as we engage with the world in a way that the other two are not. Not running with the Shame and Honour plank may be why the church often struggles to equip people to fulfil their callings outside church.
>
> On a personal level, when you get to the end of the Guilt and Innocence plank, with the message I am a sinner but I am forgiven, then the tendency is to see things as a simple question of in or out. This can encourage us to look at the rest of culture through the same lens: it's outside the kingdom and it needs to

repent. It's a simple question of in or out. It's very difficult to engage with culture on this basis. The conversation is limited. It doesn't recognise the good in culture; all it sees is black and white.

The Fear and Power plank, on the other hand, may highlight why charismatics often seem to find it difficult to engage with the world, because through that lens the world is evil and has to be overcome by out-of-the-ordinary power. So when miracles are not the everyday lived experience in the workplace, then how is God relevant, and what does my faith have to contribute to my daily tasks?

The Shame and Honour plank is different. It's a much more subtle message. It's about being on a journey towards. It's not in or out, and it's not power that needs to overwhelm. It's saying you are valuable and I am honouring who you are and what you're doing. It's saying God has deposited good stuff in you and in your culture. God loves you. So whether that's going to a small African village or going into the City and talking to bankers, it's the same point. We may acknowledge that there are things that need to fall away, but we also acknowledge that there are things to celebrate. We get to have a conversation. We get to reform incarnationally from within. It's a much more accepting and empowering space for bringing in the kingdom.'[187]

I have to say that these ideas are snapshots and caricatures of each of these three areas, but it acts as a starting point for us to think about how the gospel message, as we understand it and have imbibed it, affects the atmosphere and underlying beliefs and values of our Christian communities.

---

187. James Featherby, speaking at Network Church, 4 March 2018, https://www.networkchurch.org/Media/AllMedia.aspx (accessed 8.12.20), reworked and edited for this book.

In my view, our Western culture has shifted from one of Guilt and Innocence to that of Shame and Honour. With this in mind, not only the way we talk about the gospel but also the way we are able to include people in our Christian communities needs to be thought through and re-evaluated. In doing this we will start to bridge the gap between where the schools' work team identify the teenagers are and how their church communities are set up and organised as well as the language used.

I saw this in sharp focus whilst running a 'Friendship First' course as part of the leadership team of a local churches together initiative.[188] The Friendship First course is designed to help Christians build friendships with their Muslim neighbours. As we worked through the material and carried out the exercises together, I became increasingly aware that a bigger challenge lay ahead. The way that we had constructed our Christian communities and what our Muslim friends were looking for were potentially poles apart. Their culture was highly relational, unlike ours in the West that, generally, valued individuals and privacy. To encourage them to follow Jesus was one thing; to ask them to join the church was something else and would mean that we would have to be saved from our individualism first!

This raises a paramount issue for us, which is how responsible is it for us to reshape our message but be unwilling to reshape our Christian communities so that those who find Jesus can continue to follow him and grow in their faith. Surely, both of those things need to happen if the gospel is going to bear effective fruit. Again, we have tended to separate the two areas of evangelism and discipleship, as we have called them; these two areas will need to be joined together, and merge in our new way of thinking. In this way, evangelism will look more like discipleship.

I want to emphasise that what I am doing here is not proposing a system that needs to be followed or pretending that in any way I have all

---

188. http://friendshipfirst.org (accessed 8.12.20).

the answers to this. What follows are my musings and reflections on what I have been experimenting with in this area as we have sought to live out some of the challenges I have highlighted in a local church situation. Although much of what I share is from a leadership perspective, this does not make it solely for those in leadership; it is simply my frame of reference. I will attempt where possible to step outside that frame, or at least explain how it might look different in another context.

Chapter 22: Shame-resilient Christian Communities

I have worked consistently over the last twenty years with local churches through my partnership with Laurence Singlehurst and a faithful team, running Cell UK,[189] which encourages small groups in local churches. This has been a fascinating experience, connecting us with many churches from across the denominations and new Church streams. We have been trying to create materials and resources for the small groups that exist in local churches, helping them to have, amongst other things, a missional heartbeat.

As we have done this together, we have found ourselves highlighting an often unexplored thread that runs through the New Testament. This is the mention of the 'one another' statements. A quick online search will show you that there are some fifty-eight mentions of this phrase. Some that you may be familiar with would include, 'encouraging one another'[190] or 'Be kind and compassionate to one another'.[191]

As we continue to look at the 'one another' phrases, I want to focus particularly on how they shape and form our relationships. I have noticed that leadership is key here and needs to recognise the nature of how the community functions if these 'one another' statements are allowed to be the guiding principles around which the community is built. It is for this reason that leadership is a reoccurring theme over these next few pages. It is also the area that I have worked from whilst trying to see some of my aspirations come to reality, so I have become attuned to seeing things from my leadership perspective and so most readily describe them from that vantage point.

---

189. Cell UK Ministries, https://celluk.org.uk/ (accessed 8.12.20).
190. Hebrews 10:25.
191. Ephesians 4:32.

I realise that not everyone who reads this will have this leadership perspective, and so you may feel a little disconnected from my point of view here. However, can I ask you to think about how you carry yourself in this respect, as we often take on the characteristics of those who lead us and find ourselves operating in a similar way? We can also think about the aspirations we hold for those who lead us, and the expectations we put on them to act and respond in a certain way. So even if we do not have leadership responsibility ourselves, bear in mind what we may be expecting from those who do, and see how this is affected by the areas I highlight.

These 'one another's' show in essence how the early Church related together as one to another. This is, of course, very helpful, particularly for small groups, as in this setting in particular we tend to relate in a more free-flowing 'one another' way. In the larger settings of Sunday gatherings, this may not be as easy and, in most cases, certainly not encouraged due to the more formalised nature of our gatherings. I think these 'one another's are particularly relevant as we think about combating shame and creating, as Brené Brown puts it, 'shame resilience'. She writes:

> After fifteen years of social work education, I was sure of one thing: Connection is why we're here; it is what gives purpose and meaning to our lives. The power that connection holds in our lives was confirmed when the main concern about connection emerged as the fear of disconnection; the fear that something we've done or failed to do, something about who we are or where we come from, has made us unlovable and unworthy of connection. I learned that we resolve this concern by understanding our vulnerabilities and cultivating empathy, courage, and compassion – what I call shame resilience.[192]

---

192. Brené Brown, Appendix to *Daring Greatly*, https://brenebrown.com/the-research (accessed 8.12.20).

As Christian communities, we can be offering places of empathy, courage and compassion. I believe we can do this if we take the one another statements as our lead. This is primarily because the 'one another's' create a very strong relational culture; they are aimed at building and keeping relationships. As we will see, they push against secrecy, silence and judgement, which cause an exponential growth in shame. They encourage empathy, which is shame's very antidote. So, it is without hesitation that I want to explore them in this next section and use them as a lens through which we can look at the New Testament and allow them to shape the way we establish our 'Christian communities'. I am using this phrase 'Christian communities' rather than 'Church' as it speaks more of a relational dynamic. It will, of course, mean different things for different people, but in essence I want it to remind us that we gather together in relationship with God and each other and in this, bear witness to a watching world.

I think the 'one another's' find their initial source in the Trinitarian nature of the Godhead. They are on this basis not just a convenient way of working that the early Church developed to survive persecution, or a strategy that Jesus used to ensure that plural leadership models were developed. When we focus our Christian communities' health and life around the 'one another's, we simply yet profoundly demonstrate the heart and life of the Trinitarian relationships between the Father, Son and Holy Spirit.

We can only imagine the heartache felt as the Trinitarian relationships are reformed and Jesus is born as one of us, having left his beloved Father and the Holy Spirit. The separation is seen in its intensity as Jesus dies a painful, shameful death on the cross and cries out, 'My God, my God, why have you forsaken me?'[193] In the guilt way of thinking we reference the separation here as our guilt being borne by Jesus. However. when

---

193. Matthew 27:46.

we are thinking about shame we need to look at this differently. The shame that sends us hiding in the garden in Genesis[194] would have surely hidden and separated the Son from the Father as he died, having been made worthless by our world and its systems.

In another garden, called Gethsemane, Jesus has these telling words on his lips: 'not my will, but yours be done.'[195] Not being driven by his own ego, as we so often are, but wanting to bring honour to his Father as he engages in the most painful conversation of his life. This glimpse into the conversation within the Godhead is so revealing.

On the one hand, if we believe that Jesus came solely to die, as in that was his purpose, as it would appear many Christians do, then this conversation is a façade. Or could it be that something else was going on here, something a little more complex, perhaps? Did this conversation have authenticity to it, in that just like us, Jesus had 'say so', by which I mean the choice was legitimately open to him to spare his life at this point? Some would say that this was never an option to him, as God the Father needed him to die to save us from our sin. I would want to say, however, that this is only one perspective on what Paul describes as 'the mystery of Christ'.[196] This mystery has been simplified so as to take away any mystery and, in doing so, has made a transaction between God the Father and us, where the Son becomes the fall guy (no pun intended) in the set-up. But I digress.

What if we saw this conversation in another light, in which Jesus has 'say so' and is not compelled to follow what we interpret as a 'sovereign act of God', where God the Father is needing Jesus to die? What if Jesus has a choice here, and so the whole context for this conversation was set in a different reality? Not just an objective reality, by which I mean the parties involved are seen as standing outside the situation and looking

194. Genesis 3:8.
195. Luke 22:42.
196. Colossians 4:3.

in, which is in practice, of course, a false construct as reality has to be experienced to be real. If Jesus' reality here is to live out his life on earth 'as it is in heaven',[197] then may this conversation reflect that somehow? A life based out of relationship and built on covenant rather than individual ego, which so often defaults to a contract idea.

Jesus is living out the values he has known from all eternity within his Trinitarian community, and he brings these very values to the confines of his earthly reality of time and humanity. He is 'the Living Expression'[198] of the Godhead filled with the Holy Spirit and demonstrating the Father's heart in his every action and word.

So what could this conversation be about here in the garden, if we put aside for a moment some of our previously held views about it? What if we look at it in the light of an alternative view of reality, one shaped by a transformational view of relationships within the Trinity, rather than a transactional view of these dynamics and how they need to be played out here? What then might we see? What if the cup here, which the conversation revolves around, was not simply God the Father's cup of death for Jesus?

What if the cup here represents a choice to live out of a set of values established in the community of the Godhead? A way of working that would bring heaven to earth in this key moment? A choice by Jesus to deny the cry of the ego and instead choose 'the other'? Not to make the focus the 'one' but 'the others'? In this way, Jesus' death is not the result of a potentially vindictive father who needs to punish his son, which is often the way that many agnostics and atheists see this, even if we as believers would not necessarily put it in this stark language. Rather, it is Jesus continuing to live his life based on heavenly values, which are at odds with the world's ways. His death in this way becomes a continuation of his life. Commenting on the creed, N.T. Wright sees

---

197. Matthew 6:10, TPT.
198. John 1:14, TPT.

how this connection between Jesus, life and death has been missed, and in his words 'the middle story' is skipped over:

> ... *And was incarnate of the Holy Spirit from the Virgin Mary, and was made man.*

Then we can imagine a deep breath, a dramatic pause, as we wait to see if anything further will be said about Jesus. But no, the creed leaps right over the whole 'middle story' and lands once more at the end:

> *And was crucified also for us under Pontius Pilate ...*

... no detail at all, no *mention* at all, of anything between the second person of the Trinity becoming human and this human/divine man being 'crucified for us under Pontius Pilate.' There is nothing there about what Jesus did, or why he did it, or how anything he did relates to either his birth or his death.[199]

Jesus finds himself facing death at the hands of those who stood against the values of the kingdom of God. Here, heaven confronts earth. Jesus includes, where earthly values exclude, he 'one another's' with those who earthly dictates say you should not 'one another' with. He offers people a sense of value and purpose, just like the sense of value and purpose that he has always known in his relationships within the Trinity. This is what he is all about. Where ego is established or reinforced at the expense of the 'other', it is contrary to kingdom values that are underpinned by our sense of identity being found in and through our relationship with God. Our very personhood, just as those of the Trinity, is established through our relationships caught up in the Trinity and in the life that flows between us as believers as we live out the 'one another's.

So, the Trinitarian nature of God is our starting point as we consider the 'one another' statements and the challenges they bring to us as we live

---

199. N.T. Wright, *How God Became King: The Forgotten Story of the Gospels* (London: HarperCollins, 2012), Kindle edition, location 356.

out a more intentionally relational life in our Christian communities. I am indebted to Roger Forster, who speaks and writes so passionately about the relational dynamics of our Trinitarian God, and has inspired and influenced me greatly in this respect.[200]

The 'one another's give us a very valuable insight into the way the early Church worked and, in particular, provide by default an insight into the forms and styles of early Church leadership that were created in these local Christian communities. The fact that they are 'one another' statements in itself identifies a horizontal connection across these communities that is not leader-centric. We often superimpose on the New Testament our experience of leadership and assume that it worked the same in their context. I will undoubtedly do some of that in my writing here, as we all come with our preconceptions. My hope is that through this exploration of how the 'one another's might act as a shaping influence in our Christian communities, we will come to see how our leadership roles may need to be reshaped and reformed. In this way, we can help create environments where we can experience the dynamic participation and transformational impact of those early communities, and see them become a reality for us in the twenty-first century.

In this way, we will help to shape 'shame-resilient' communities. As people participate, they find their voice and a sense of value through belonging. They will find a place where unhelpful secrets can be uncovered and loving acceptance fostered.

So let's take a few moments to look at what it might mean for our communities to be formed around these 'one another' statements.

---

200. Roger Forster, *Trinity* (Milton Keynes: Authentic Media, 2004).

Chapter 23: The Anybody and Everybody Movement

I have often wondered why so much of the ministry in Church is done by the leaders? Why are they so centre stage; in fact, why is there a stage at all? I thought the age of the Spirit, inaugurated on the day of Pentecost, was a shift towards every-member ministry, where God says, 'I will pour out my Spirit on all people. Your sons and daughters will prophesy, your young men will see visions, your old men will dream dreams. Even on my servants, both men and women, I will pour out my Spirit in those days, and they will prophesy.'[201]

This pouring out of the Spirit starts a new era, a move towards the coming of the kingdom of God through the lives of those who believe in and follow Jesus. This anybody and everybody movement includes 'servants, both men and women'. So we have moved from 'particular people doing particular things at particular times'[202] to everybody who follows God being indwelt and empowered by his Spirit. There is a thread that leads us through the New Testament that shows us the reality of how this was lived out amongst the early Church. This thread is made up of the fifty-eight 'one another' statements, as I have already highlighted. People empowered by the Holy Spirit, living in relationship with each other and sharing ministry together. No stage, no lights, but a load of action! Quite a bit of drama and, I am sure, some heartache along the way, not to mention some mayhem. However, this was real life and all those components and many more besides are the reality of life.

So the fifty-eight 'one another's' of the New Testament paint a picture for us of life in the early Church, as Bill Beckham so helpfully describes

---

201. Acts 2:17-18.
202. Nicky Gumbel, 'Who is the Holy Spirit?', *Alpha Manual* (London: Alpha International, 2011; second revised edition), p. 31.

it, as meaning 'being responsible to and for one another'.[203] It is this sense of mutual responsibility that has come in for a degree of judgement and, at the very least, suspicion by many in leadership, as well as a good number of those who are part of our congregations. Although not voiced necessarily in these terms, a degree of unease is expressed when this 'one another' idea is proposed. Often though it is not even on our radar. Let me give you an example of a situation where I bumped into a reluctance to operate from the 'one another' principle. You may start to notice similar things as you let these ideas settle in your mind.

At a breakfast meeting, I was asked if I would take on the role of leading the 'ministry team' for the men's event which we were organising as a joint churches initiative. The person who had suggested this, and run it for the first event, could no longer be involved. I paused, picked up my coffee and found myself explaining why this would not be something I would be entirely comfortable with. I said that I would be very happy to lead any response time by suggesting that the men prayed for and with each other and I could facilitate this in a way that helped everyone that was willing to participate.

John Wimber's words echoed in my mind: 'Everyone gets to play',[204] or in this case, pray. Memories came back to me of the slightly chaotic scene from a meeting that, as I recall, John himself spoke at and his team led in my old school hall one evening. He was invited by a local church, during one of his visits to the UK. Invites went out for anyone who wanted to come along and hear him speak. I was in my late teens and went with a couple of friends to see what it was all about. After he had spoken, he asked the Holy Spirit to come and use us to minister to each other. It was a truly amazing experience to be part of that. I think it spoilt me for anything less!

203. William A. Beckham, teaching on small groups in 2001, High Leigh Conference Centre, Hertfordshire.
204. John Wimber, *Everyone Gets to Play* (Garden City, ID: Ampelon Publishing, 2013).

Several things came to mind as I reflected on my response to the question over breakfast, a day or two later. Firstly, I was the obvious candidate to ask to lead the 'ministry team' at the event for a group of businessmen. As a church leader, I would do the 'spiritual work'. Now, this is something that I recognise I can do and is part of my role, but I also strongly believe this is something we *all* can and should be encouraged to do. The idea of the 'priesthood of all believers', whilst a doctrinal statement, is often not very evident in our practice. As part of our breakfast conversation, I was described as the person who believed in every member ministry, which I took as a compliment and agreed that I certainly did. What the conversation highlighted, however, was the fact that although this was my particular belief, it was not everyone's. So the default to the leaders doing the spiritual work was alive and well in this situation, as is so often the case. If we did a poll, I am sure most Christian leaders would put their hands up to believing in the priesthood of all believers as a statement of faith. The difficulty seems to come in translating it into practical reality. This is, to some degree, due to the fact that leadership tends to be described in terms that puts it firmly in the 'doing the ministry' space. Leadership has adopted the names that convey this, the most obvious being 'the minister'; this pushes right back into the 'particular people' territory mentioned earlier. In doing this we automatically exclude everyone else; they can then feel 'less than', somehow inferior or unworthy, one of the roots of shame.

Secondly, I wanted to challenge the very thought that we needed a ministry team in the first place. Our earlier conversations about setting this men's group up had focused on the need to challenge men to step up and step out in their faith. We had, however, defaulted to a disempowering model of operation where a handful of 'specially chosen' people would be involved in the 'prayer ministry team'. This default to having 'specially selected people' doing things is very strongly built into church life and pushes hard against the 'one another' idea. This is compounded by the way modernity has worked, creating areas of specialism that from a manufacturing and business organisation point of view makes good sense. However, when it comes to church life which, in my view, needs to be seen more as family than organisation, we need to rethink some of the categories we work out of and, in particular, where we apply them. Obviously, we all have different gifts and need to have space to use them, and it is this space to use them that most concerns me as so often the spaces are shut down or ring-fenced for specific people who somehow 'qualify' to minister. This, in my mind, is often a denial of the New Testament mandate for 'every member ministry'. I explore this area more in Chapter 31, when I look at the out working of the Ephesians' four gifts, and how they are to be seen in an every member context rather than as solely leadership gifts.

Thirdly, I realised that I was not declining to lead, but that my offer of leadership was not on the basis of 'doing the ministry' but rather facilitating all those that wanted to be involved. It's often easier and less risky to just do it yourself, but in my experience far more productive to encourage others. I have formulated a little joke when people introduce me as their pastor. I say, 'Yes, is that pastor with carbonara sauce!' This reminds them that I am not very comfortable with the title, as it strongly suggests that I am the *one* that does all the pastoring. I am similarly uncomfortable with being called 'the minister' as this has even stronger connotations that I am the *one* who does the ministry, which flies straight in the face of 'every-member ministry'. I recall being asked to go and talk to a leadership team some years ago; they were struggling to get people involved in ministry in the church. They had a congregation of some 200 people and I met with their 'ministry staff team' of six, employed people. It was a delicate situation, as to some degree the team sat around me having lunch and chatting were the very cause of the problem. They had been employed by the congregation to 'do the ministry'; they had become the 'special people' who could do the ministry, so why should the members of the congregation do it themselves?

What happens, in my view, in these situations is that those in leadership hog the growing space. What I mean by this is that we grow as followers of Jesus by practising to do the things that Jesus did. This is how discipleship works. So practising what Jesus did is for every one of us. When we as leaders do most of the ministry, then there is little or no space for others to practise and grow. We as leaders hold onto the growing space rather than giving it away and enabling those we lead to grow themselves and others by occupying this space. That's not to say we make ourselves redundant, but rather think of our leadership role as that of a coach enabling others to be involved on the field of play.

Chapter 24: Helping People Thrive

One of my favourite 'one another' verses is Colossians 3:16: 'Let the message of Christ dwell among you richly as you teach and admonish one another with all wisdom through psalms, hymns, and songs from the Spirit, singing to God with gratitude in your hearts.'

The area of teaching is often one that is most guarded by leadership. Now, I understand that this may be for good reasons, but how can this verse find its proper fulfilment amongst us if we don't open our pulpits? So at Network Church I use my leadership to expand the space that would traditionally be reserved for me as the leader to teach in. I deliberately open it up for others. I am constantly on the lookout for those who have something to teach us. Many of them would not rush to the front or want to share what they have, so part of my role is to find ways to make that possible for them. In doing this we have a whole variety of people in front of us Sunday by Sunday and in our small groups. This enables us to experience the diversity of Jesus' body through its members. I find that as people share from their particular perspectives, others are able to connect with them more readily. They feel understood and receive teaching and encouragement that is relevant to them specifically. In this way, their sense of belonging is increased as they feel more understood and connected. All this helps to transform any sense of shame that they may be carrying.

During a conversation with one of our small-group leaders, I heard about how good someone was at leading the Word section in their group where they looked at and applied the Bible together. I make a mental note of these things and the next time we are putting together our teaching rota for Sundays, I will ask if the person in question would be willing to consider speaking one Sunday. Another way that this happens is during conversations with people. Maybe they have been challenged by something, and have been working it through with God and are telling you all about it; it becomes obvious that this is an area they have reflected on and battled in. They have valuable insights to share and lessons they have learned. It is a relatively short step from here to helping them bring these insights to the congregation so we can all learn together and benefit from their encounter with God through their challenges.

I think this can also be effective if the situation they are grappling with has not been completely resolved, as this demonstrates the reality that we live with. In this way, we will all benefit from their insight, wisdom and experience of God and his Word in the midst of the situation. This means that they often share in a more vulnerable way, highlighting some of their uncertainty and even doubt about what God is up to in the challenges they are facing. This often means that what is expressed as they speak exposes the reality and often complexity of any given situation. This exposure of reality uncovers areas that we may be tempted to keep secret until we have resolved them, and allows us to overcome the silence that is often kept around these things because we feel they are messy and unresolved. In this way, we are overturning the secrecy, silence and ultimately judgement that we may fear, which if you remember, are the three things that Brené Brown's research shows causes shame to grow exponentially. There is, of course, a need to make sure that the areas shared on these occasions are suitable for this slightly more public setting. We often choose not to make these more 'family' feeling talks available on our website as this also encourages greater participation if time is given to discussion, as well as making the person speaking feel more at ease about what they are saying.

As well as all of the above, the person speaking will grow as they prepare and share their insights with us. Those who take up the challenge tell me that although they may find it pushes them out of their comfort zone, the benefits are enormous. They grow in confidence and often find themselves transferring the skills they learn here to other situations in the workplace or social settings. Not everyone wants to teach in the same way, and are sometimes put off by thinking that they have to conform to a pattern. So, part of my role is to talk through with them how they can teach in a way that works best for them.

Let me give you a couple of examples here. More artistic people sometimes find it difficult to get their thoughts into a logical order, so time spent listening and helping them structure what they want to bring is often helpful in this sort of situation. One particular lady called Rydal wanted to have her hands completely free and needed to draw her thoughts in pictures, so we devised a scheme together where she produced her notes on lining paper, the sort that you hang on the wall before painting or papering over them when decorating a room. She produced the notes in the form of pictures that she drew. This was then rolled out on the floor, stuck down with masking tape and she simply walked along it, talking about the pictures as she went, unrestricted and hands-free. She was comfortable working in this way and we got the benefit of being able to follow not only what she said, but the actions that brought it to life as she moved along the lining paper with her hands completely free so she could express herself fully.[205]

Others have found it helpful to have me share the space with them; in this way I act as a bit of a safety net and they are not standing on their own. This will often take the form of being more like an interview, with me asking clarifying questions and drawing out of them what they have already shared with me in private, but now in a more public setting. In this way, I am offering servant leadership as I am trying to serve them by creating a space in which they can minister to us all, such that we can all grow together.

One of the things that makes this shared pulpit possible is being available myself to step in at the last minute if someone can't make it

---

205. http://www.rydalhanbury.com/ (accessed 11.10.21).

as planned, or gets cold feet. Knowing there is a back-up plan is really helpful. This is good both for them, as it takes the pressure off, and for all of us, as we know that things will continue. So, part of carrying my responsibility as a leader is to act as the backstop in these situations. This means holding your nerve and being willing to be flexible. It also demands that we shift the teaching space away from performance and take the competitive nature of the task out of the picture.

One of the reasons this is able to work as I have described is that our weekly small groups encourage participation. This means that people are used to contributing, hearing the sound of their own voice and putting into words what they experience of God. This may sound obvious, but it's amazing how often in small groups this does not happen. Also, it's interesting to see how many people in churches are not even in a small group so would never even get the opportunity to participate even if it was offered. Even here, though, the voice of the small-group leader can become dominant. In this small-group situation, it may not be the main church leader's voice that dominates, those who lead these small groups often take their lead in style and purpose from the Sunday meeting and so can have a tendency to dominate the space. So, once again we need to be intentional as to the role of leadership, to encourage atmospheres of participation which in turn will encourage growth as people have space to do 'the ministry' themselves, rather than just be ministered to. This acts as a weekly reminder in these groups that we all have value, and have things to offer into these groups. Proving that far from there being 'something wrong me' as the shame script suggests, there is something very right with us as we find we are listened to, encouraged, and get to have a say. It's such a thrill to see others in the group respond as someone tentatively shares for the first time; it often seems to me that the Holy Spirit is more at work in these situations.

Joel Comiskey, writing about small-group leadership, encourages us to re think what it looks like:

I use the word leader with some reservation because of its connotation of position and power. In some cultures, for example, a leader is a person who controls and dominates. Many people believe that a 'Christian leader' automatically holds an official position in the church. A new consensus, however, has developed that defines the word leader with one word: influence. When I use the word leader, I am referring to a person who exercises his or her God-given capacity to influence a specific group of God's people toward God's purposes for the group. I often interchange the word leader with facilitator, because the best small group leaders encourage participation by the members of the group.[206]

You might get the impression that I am having a go at leaders. That is not my aim here, I believe wholeheartedly in good leadership. I just think in light of where our culture is and, in particular, what we have said about the shame epidemic, we need to re-evaluate how we see leadership and its role in our Christian communities.

My current definition of leadership would be something like 'those involved in creating environments where people thrive'. This not only shifts the perspective of what leadership is about, it also broadens the scope because we can all have a part to play in creating places where we all thrive. We need to be careful that we don't create environments where people feel that they are silenced and judged, which as we have already mentioned, are two of the causes of shame. For more about how these shame-resilient environments can be created and sustained, I recommend Brené Brown's book *Dare to Lead*.[207]

---

206. Joel Comiskey, *The Spirit-filled Small Group* (Edmond, OK: CCS Publishing, 2013), p. 4.
207. Brené Brown, *Dare to Lead: Brave Work. Tough Conversations. Whole Hearts* (London: Vermilion, 2018).

Food for thought

Here are a few practical things we can think about as we reflect on our Christian communities and how we can create spaces for people to step out and grow in the 'one another's', in the belief that as we engage in these 'one another's' together we will value each other and in so doing make space for each other to find acceptance and appreciation, and so minimise the shame that causes separation and a sense of worthlessness.

Creating atmospheres of growth

One of our challenges is to create atmospheres of growth. Environments where people find it easy to 'have a go', to step out, and as a result, be better equipped to discover and use their core gifts that have so often been buried or underutilised through life; to become more fully those who God created them to be.

So, what creates these environments?

Many of us have travelled quite a distance in our own development, but seldom take the opportunity to share in an open and vulnerable way what that has been like for us. So, as with many things, it starts with us sharing our experiences of growth honestly, including the ups and downs. This really helps to break the silence that contributes to shame that is often caused by the need to be seen to get things right. For instance, our stories are often only told when they have a good and sorted ending. Whilst we need the encouragement of hearing these stories, we also need the balance of hearing the reality of our lives where things don't always work out in the way we hoped. In this way we come out of hiding in the pretence that everything is fine and that we have life sorted, because in truth, much of the time it doesn't feel that way, if we are honest.

A culture of experimentation

Many people in our churches believe that they can't 'have a go' at something until they have got everything sorted. We are used to hearing, 'I won't be able to help someone else until I have got my act together completely.' Our theology sometimes does not help us here as we often view failure as sin, as for so many the Christian life is about 'getting it right'. I am regularly challenged by the words 'go and … surely I am with you always' from Matthew's Gospel [208] - it's as we step out that we experience God with us, as we go. It's a well-known fact that we seldom get things right the first time, so we need to create opportunities for 'having a go'. James Dyson, now the very well-known designer of the bagless vacuum cleaner, spent five years perfecting his idea. There were 5,127 prototypes before he created the world's first vacuum cleaner that was bagless, the DC01.[209]

Small groups are, of course, great incubators for people to have a go. This raises a question for me. Do we have a theology of experimentation? By this, I mean is it all right for us to try something and believe that God will work on it and in it with us, without the need for us to get it 'right first time'? A God who meets us in our failure, who empathises with our weakness? I think if we are honest, deep down, many of us fear getting things wrong and feeling guilty, which has historically been drummed into us, and as such are finding it difficult to adjust our way of thinking to having a go and believing we might indeed find God in the failure as well as the success of our attempts.

A need for encouragement

Here is another of the 'one another' statements: 'Therefore, encourage one another and build each other up, just as in fact you are doing.'[210]

---

208. Matthew 28:18-20.
209. James Dyson, 'The Accidental Engineer', https://www.jamesdysonfoundation. co.uk/who-we-are/our-story.html (accessed 8.12.20).
210. 1 Thessalonians 5:11.

I am constantly amazed what a little positive encouragement can do. When did you last enable someone to step out of their comfort zone and try something new? It needs to be a regular part of our rhythm to build people up through words of encouragement. We can all do this just as Hebrews says: 'And let us consider how we may spur one another on towards love and good deeds, not giving up meeting together, as some are in the habit of doing, but encouraging one another –and all the more as you see the Day approaching.' [211] A word of warning here, in that it is essential to be genuine and specific, otherwise we come across as bland and insincere, giving away praise lightly. This has the opposite effect, as it devalues you and the person you are wanting to encourage, and does very little to push against the shame that traps us in seeing ourselves as less than we are.

Always looking for potential

Try playing a little scenario game. Every time you meet someone, look for their untapped potential; what is it that God sees in them that is being overlooked? Some clues are to see what they get passionate or excited about; what brings them alive that is not yet being outworked in their life? What is in the embryonic stage of development that just needs fanning into flame?[212] Let's be amongst those who are cheering others on, seeing the race marked out for them and helping them run it well. In doing this we will see these familiar words from Hebrews become more of a reality: 'Therefore, since we are surrounded by such a great cloud of witnesses, let us throw off everything that hinders and the sin that so easily entangles. And let us run with perseverance the race marked out for us.'[213]

---

211. Hebrews 10:24-25.
212. 2 Timothy 1:6.
213. Hebrews 12:1.

Sorting the issues

For many, there are good reasons why they don't want to step out and grow. Are we prepared to put the work in, to build trusting relationships and discover some of the obstacles to growth? Sometimes previous hurts and failures have not been dealt with well, and we need to walk with each other through a healing process so we are willing to have another go. Solid friendships, which take an investment of time, are often what is needed here. Friendships where we feel we can trust each other and be brave enough to open up about past hurts and seek health and healing. Through empathising with and helping each other, we experience God at work through his Spirit in us as we see these past obstacles overcome and people set free from the secrecy, silence and judgement that has help them captive to shame. This often happens little by little and it is good to reflect and mark the progress along the way.

Chapter 25: Creating Space for People

This is where a small group really comes into its own. In a group I attend regularly, I was down to lead the welcome part at the beginning of our time together. This normally took the form of a question that we all then answered in turn around the group. This is a simple idea but very effective, as it gets everyone speaking and used to hearing the sound of their own voice in the group.[214] On this occasion I asked, 'What new skill would you like to learn?' The answers were varied and, in some cases, quite surprising. However, even by verbalising them to each other we created the possibility that they may happen. I even went on a well-known auction website to try and bid for a woodworking lathe for one of the group (sadly I was outbid), but wouldn't it have been fun to have arrived at the group next week with a surprise present!

1 Corinthians 14:26-33 says:

> What then shall we say, brothers and sisters? When you come together, each of you has a hymn, or a word of instruction, a revelation, a tongue or an interpretation. Everything must be done so that the church may be built up. If anyone speaks in a tongue, two – or at the most three – should speak, one at a time, and someone must interpret. If there is no interpreter, the speaker should keep quiet in the church and speak to himself and to God. Two or three prophets should speak, and the others should weigh carefully what is said. And if a revelation comes to someone who is sitting down, the first speaker should stop. For you can all prophesy in turn so that everyone may be instructed and encouraged. The spirits of prophets are subject to the control

214. For more on helpful small-group patterns that encourage participation, see Laurence Singlehurst, *Small Groups: An Introduction* (Harpenden: Cell UK Ministries, 2017), https://celluk.org.uk/ (accessed 8.12.20).

of prophets. For God is not a God of disorder but of peace – as in all the congregations of the Lord's people.

These verses are often used to bring discipline to what appear to be unruly gatherings, but it is worth reflecting on what was quite normal for the church in Corinth. The words here say when you come together, 'each of you has a hymn' etc. It does not say those that have completed such and such a training course or received specific instruction, it simply says 'each of you'. It was taken as read that everyone would bring a contribution and it would be unusual if that did not happen. Participation was the norm, leading to the need for Paul to help them make this work in a more orderly fashion. He doesn't say this is all wrong, you should not all be participating like this. He encourages them to participate and helps them to do it in a way that they can all be 'built up'. This building up is essential in our specific context as we are thinking about shame. Shame knocks us down it devalues us and it excludes us. We need this 'building up' to counteract the feelings of being knocked down and devalued. Of all places, our Christian communities should be places where we are built up! I think those in the early Church that Paul is writing about are built up in two specific ways.

Firstly, as I have already outlined, they are built up by contributing and expressing those things that God has laid on their hearts to bring. This very expression of their faith in making their contribution builds them up as individuals, it strengthens them in their faith as they experience God and see his Holy Spirit working through them. They are encouraged further as they witness others responding and actively engaging with their contribution. In this way, we experience very directly God's validation of who we are as he uses us and our particular gifts. This says you are worth God using you, he is choosing to use you because he loves you and wants to see you drawn closer to him as you step out. This validation we receive from the Father confirms that he loves us as sons and daughters; any shame that we carry will be thrown off as we experience God's love and power working through us in this way.

M. Scott Peck puts this in the context of love so well as he writes:

Love was defined as, 'the will to extend one's self for the purpose of nurturing one's own or another's spiritual growth'. When we grow, it is because we are working at it, and we are working at it because we love ourselves. It is through love that we elevate ourselves. And it is through love our love for others that we assist others to elevate themselves.[215]

This is such a good insight from Peck. It highlights the multidimensional nature of our participation through extending ourselves in love. It both helps us and those we are reaching out to.

Secondly, in the passage, they themselves are built up and edified, as they receive and respond to what others in the gathering are offering. This two-way flow is very descriptive of the 'one another' statements. Being responsible to and for 'one another'. There is often a tangible sense of God's leading in this sort of environment as one thing leads to another and God's voice is heard through the whole body. In this way, we are leading 'one another' in response to what God is doing in each of us by his Holy Spirit.

In this context of leading one another, we could consider Hebrews 12:15: 'See to it that no one falls short of the grace of God and that no bitter root grows up to cause trouble and defile many'. In place of 'See to it' other translations use 'Looking diligently' (KJV) or 'Look after each other' (NLT). Zens notes:

The verb episcope is used here, but is totally lost in most English translations. The author is saying 'take the oversight' of one another. Here is a 'leadership' verb used elsewhere of 'overseers' (elders), but is here being applied as a responsibility of the

215. M. Scott Peck, *The Road Less Travelled* (London: Arrow Books, 1990), p. 286.

whole body. So, again, if a group of Christians cannot from their inception grow in their functioning as a priesthood of mutual overseers, how can we ever expect some future overseers to arise as servants to the body?[216]

This sheds a whole new light on the idea of leadership and, in particular, oversight. It takes it out of its often overbearing and restricting definitions and puts it in the rather liberating place of the 'one another's.

Most importantly, however, it liberates oversight from the realm of a few and makes it the task of the many. We become responsible to and for each other. This could be seen by some as madness, leading to chaos, except that we have the Holy Spirit dwelling in each of us, to lead and guide us in this respect. We therefore need to lift our heads, to put our hope in the God who sees each of our potential, the one who looks beyond the shame we carry. In this way, we will see more clearly the resources placed in the body of Christ. This is not to deny the place of leadership, but to redefine its scope and purpose in respect to enabling the body to work together and so represent Jesus to a watching world.

For a few years I played a little game with those new to Network Church; it was called 'spot the leaders'. One particular individual took it very seriously as leadership was very important to him. Sadly, this was due to a few 'run ins' with leaders over the course of his life in a number of other local churches before arriving with us. It took him several months to spot the five members of the leadership team in Network at that time. This was not because they were low in profile, but rather because so many others in the life of the church took upfront roles and generally participated in our Sunday gatherings as God prompted them, and in doing so, looked like leaders.

---

216. Jon H. Zens, *58 to 0: How Christ Leads Through the One Anothers* (Omaha, NE: Ekklesia Press), p. 17.

We have often assumed that the New Testament was written to leaders. We have subconsciously excluded ourselves as members of the body of Christ from ministry activities because we think that is what leaders do. In this way, we can easily read the New Testament through what I call a leadership lens. It is as if we put on glasses that shape everything we read, to look as if it was written to and about those who lead. Jon Zens picks this up as he writes, 'I don't think we have begun to grasp the significance of the fact that the N.T [sic] letters were written to *ekklesias* [The whole Church], not leaders. As I pointed out above, the writer of Hebrews told all of the Lord's people to "oversee one another" using a "leadership" verb from which we get our English word "Episcopal". So what I am attempting to highlight here is that there is an unhealthy reliance and focus on leadership in its classic form. Zens goes on to explain further:

> There is a leader centric approach to our church constructs and operational practice. 'The way of Jesus stands diametrically opposed to this paradigm.'[217]

We need to remind ourselves that Jesus is 'the head of his body';[218] he is in ultimate leadership, as it were. Paul reminds us of this in Ephesians when he talks about how the body works together:

> Then we will no longer be infants, tossed back and forth by the waves, and blown here and there by every wind of teaching and by the cunning and craftiness of people in their deceitful scheming. Instead, speaking the truth in love, we will grow to become in every respect the mature body of him who is the head, that is, Christ. From him the whole body, joined and held together by every supporting ligament, grows and builds itself up in love, as each part does its work.[219]

---

217. Zens, *58 to 0: How Christ leads through the One Anothers*, pp. 17,20.
218. Colossians 1:18.
219. Ephesians 4:14-16.

We are called to be the body of Christ under his headship, to continue his work on the earth. He has equipped us to do this by returning to the Father and sending his Holy Spirit to indwell and empower us. He says:

> I will ask the Father, and he will give you another advocate to help you and be with you for ever – the Spirit of truth. The world cannot accept him, because it neither sees him nor knows him. But you know him, for he lives with you and will be in you. I will not leave you as orphans; I will come to you. Before long, the world will not see me any more, but you will see me. Because I live, you also will live. On that day you will realise that I am in my Father, and you are in me, and I am in you.[220]

I think it's worth pausing at this point and just re-reading those verses and letting them sink in. There is a real danger that we have become familiar with the theoretical ideas expressed here, but not really taken the time to look at what these concepts mean in practice.

So, what do we do with these verses? We can say, 'Well, this is Jesus speaking to his disciples, they became leaders in his movement and therefore this is about leaders and addressed to them.' That may go on in our heads as we read it at some level. Or we can put this in the context of Joel's prophecy as we see the outworking of these verses in Acts 2 as Peter addresses the crowd:

> Fellow Jews and all of you who live in Jerusalem, let me explain this to you; listen carefully to what I say. These people are not drunk, as you suppose. It's only nine in the morning! No, this is what was spoken by the prophet Joel: 'In the last days, God says, I will pour out my Spirit on all people. Your sons and daughters will prophesy, your young men will see visions, your old men will

---

220. John 14:16-20.

dream dreams. Even on my servants, both men and women, I will pour out my Spirit in those days, and they will prophesy.[221]

We see then that the practical outworking of Jesus sending His Spirit is totally inclusive, it is not dependent on status, age or gender. It is not designed to devalue or exclude anyone, it is carried by the same Spirit that caused Jesus to say: 'The Spirit of the Lord is on me, because he has anointed me to proclaim good news to the poor. He has sent me to proclaim freedom for the prisoners and recovery of sight for the blind, to set the oppressed free, to proclaim the year of the Lord's favour.'[222]

Those who had been excluded because they were poor, or prisoners, blind, or oppressed can now join in. Our shame can make us poor as we are isolated from others; we are prisoners to the way we see ourselves as unworthy and can be blind in how we see others.

The outworking of Joel's prophecy continues as we see the people's response to these words as Peter explains what is going on. 'Those who accepted his message were baptised, and about three thousand were added to their number that day.'[223] These 3,000 baptisms would have been a lengthy process, had it been carried out through a leader-centric view, as we would anticipate that Peter would have baptised them all, as the preaching leader. This could not have been the case as they were all baptised 'that day'. Yet another example of the 'one another's, as they would probably have all been involved in initiating each other into this newly formed community as they were baptised.

221. Acts 2:14-18.
222. Luke 4:18-19.
223. Acts 2:41.

Chapter 26: Leading on the Edge Between Chaos and Order

Our challenge, then, should we accept it, is to live and learn to lead on this edge. The edge between chaos and order. Not a comfortable place always, but a rewarding one, as this is where life exists in all its fullness. Have you ever wondered what type of leadership lay behind the 1 Corinthians 14 passage that we looked at earlier? Let's remind ourselves of it again:

> What then shall we say, brothers and sisters? When you come together, each of you has a hymn, or a word of instruction, a revelation, a tongue or an interpretation. Everything must be done so that the church may be built up.[224]

We could think of this sense of plural leadership to some degree as holding the balance between order and chaos.

What happens here is that we push into the realm of creativity and chaos to extend the boundaries of our known space. In this way, we enlarge the kingdom. What Paul is doing through this instruction is establishing ways through order that can allow God's purposes to become apparent to the gathered community as they minister together, taking responsibility to and for each other.

> Order can become excessive, and that's not good, but chaos can swamp us, so we drown – and that is also not good. We need to stay on the straight and narrow path ... 'There' is the dividing line between order and chaos. That's where we are simultaneously stable enough, exploring enough, transforming enough, repairing

---

224. 1 Corinthians 14:26.

enough, and cooperating enough. It's there we find the meaning that justifies life and its inevitable suffering.[225]

Our temptation both as leaders and as participants is to close these spaces down too quickly, and not trust the process enough. We are often chaos averse, we quickly feel uncomfortable, fragile and to some degree out of control of the situation and therefore open to attack. We feel, to use Peterson's language, that 'chaos can swamp us'. This is a very natural response; our senses are heightened in these situations and we want to use our leadership power to regain control, or if we are not in a leadership position, we get very fearful and put pressure on leaders to do something.

However, as I say regularly to those who join me in our pottery studio, 'You can't be creative without making a mess.' Something I remind myself of when our daughter has been making cakes in the kitchen! Our creative creator God who makes us in his image is not afraid of the messy process of creation. If he was, then he would not have created us with the free will that makes this creativity possible.

Riding this space of uncertainty between order and chaos is our challenge. If we are not riding this space, I would question if we are really leading, as I think in principle this is one of the key areas that we need to work with. We are leading when we are pushing the boundaries, creating a certain amount of chaos and then establishing patterns that enable this chaos to become part of what we are extending without bringing the whole into collapse. In opening up this space we are allowing others to contribute and encouraging their voices be heard. We are saying everyone has a valuable contribution, and in doing so we are pushing actively against the shame that so many of us carry. As we hear from each other, we realise that we are not alone in the struggles we face;

---

225. Peterson, *12 Rules for Life: An Antidote to Chaos*, p. xxxiv.

we find empathy (the antidote to shame) as others step into the space with us and acknowledge their struggles with life.

Alan Mann in *Atonement for a 'Sinless' Society* looks at the power of story and says:

> Narrative, or the desire to tell stories about the world or ourselves, is the mode by which people try to make sense of the one life they have. … while narrative (or ontological) coherence may be desired, many people live, or merely 'exist', with a narrative incoherence – a breakdown in the story they are able to tell, which results in the disruption of the self.[226]

So, having places where we are heard and understood, where we are valued enough to be listened to gives us an opportunity to tell our story and in doing so, with the help of others, can bring coherence back and so help to restore the disruption of self that Mann highlights.

The other area we run into here is the role that organisation plays. To mitigate against the feeling of anarchy that chaos can bring, we can be tempted to escape into organisation.

> It is true that organising is a solution to chaos. Indeed, that is the primary reason for organisation: to minimise chaos. The trouble is, however, that organisation and community are also incompatible. Committees and chair people do not a community make. I am not implying that it is impossible for a business, church, or some other organisation to have a degree of community within itself. I am not an anarchist. But an organisation is able to nurture a measure of community within itself only to the extent that it is willing to risk or tolerate a certain lack of structure. As long as the goal is community-building, organisation as an attempted solution to chaos is an unworkable solution.[227]

---

226. Mann, *Atonement for a 'Sinless' Society*, p. 64.
227. Scott M. Peck, *The Different Drum* (London: Arrow Books, 1990), p. 93.

I found Peck's description of this tension very helpful and it brings in another dynamic that is at play when we are thinking about shame, which is the role that organisation can play in both inducing and creating shame. As a sense of community is developed, it will probably express itself in terms of family, referencing the biblical language in this respect as it is formed. The degree to which any organisation within this community space is implemented will have far-reaching consequences on the level of well-being that is experienced by those who belong. As Peck points out, there needs to be a 'certain lack of structure' for community to thrive.

The word 'community' is overused and applied to all sorts of situations. I remember someone describing a database of names on a computer as a community! In this context, as we are looking at shame-resilient communities, it is the relational connection that is key. A place where we can belong and find acceptance. A place where we can grow in our appreciation and understanding of each other and the God we serve. In this way, we will not be found needing to hide, or keep secrets for fear of being judged, which all compound shame and cause it to grow, but rather we can find empathy and acceptance, the very antidote to shame. I am reminded here of yet another of those one another statements, this time from the book of Romans, 'Accept one another, then, just as Christ accepted you ...'[228] I hope we are beginning to see how important these 'one another' verses are for us as we look at shame-resilient communities.

Jesus spends much of his time working with chaos, pushing against the accepted boundaries of his day, offering a different set of beliefs and values. This stirred things up and certainly caused a degree of chaos in the lives of those he encountered, not to mention the communities that had often excluded them. He was often surrounded by controversy, finally meeting death head-on, as the culture of his day could not cope

---

228. Romans 15:7.

with the degree of change in their mindset that he proposed; this created too much chaos for them. This brings a very real insight to Jordan Peterson's words; talking about this chaos he says, 'It's there we find the meaning that justifies life and its inevitable suffering.' So in this space, just as Jesus did, we can expect to find suffering. Probably not to the degree that he experienced it, but for certain, it will be there as part of straddling the divide between order and chaos. Are we prepared for that potential suffering, or are we just looking for the easy option? If it's the easy option we seek, then I think we need to ask ourselves if we are really growing at all, or are we just following the status quo and managing a current reality rather than developing, and in so doing, expanding the boundaries of the kingdom?

From the very earliest days in my attempts to lead in a church setting, I have always wanted to encourage this sense of participation and mutual contribution. I love the creative space that chaos often brings, the buzz of thinking on your feet and relying on God, seeing where he will lead, and what he wants to say through any given group. I think this is also due to the fact that I find others' thoughts and ideas intriguing and stimulating and, as I have said on a number of occasions, slightly tongue-in-cheek, 'I know what I think, it's far more interesting to hear what you think.' Similarly, I recall in my late teens having the occasional opportunity to lead worship with my guitar during the service in the Baptist church I attended. During this time, I would give opportunity for people in the congregation to come and share from the front as part of the worship. The only other time when people could share events from their lives happened at baptismal services, where the candidates shared their testimony of why they were getting baptised. For me, creating these opportunities was vital, as although I would not have thought it through at the time, it brought the reality of our lives into the often rather disconnected place that our Sunday worship occupied.

As I continued to think about how we could hear more from each other in our Christian communities, and in particular, started experimenting with styles of team and leadership models, I have loved and been influenced by the work of Margaret Wheatley. She is a renowned author who studies and writes about organisational behaviour with a focus on how these groups can self-organise and the leadership required to make this happen.

Wheatley comments on the need for participation and in particular its effects on a community as they bring their interpretations of any given situation. Her work has been seminal over several decades in unearthing principles from quantum physics that reveal a previously hidden world that is self-organising in its design. She contrasts this quantum world with that of the more accepted Newtonian worldview that many of our institutions and organisations have been established around. Her experiences of working with a wide variety of situations over this time make her a voice to listen to and respect. It is no wonder that the world she has discovered and writes about reflects much of our New Testament understanding of participation, co-ownership and shared responsibility, as it is the same designer behind both the natural world and the New Testament communities. Knowing that Jesus was, and is, foundational in creating the universe, it should come as no surprise that he establishes the same values and principles that we find there in the way he calls his people to participate together in their shared new life of the kingdom. Wheatley's description here is an inspiring picture of what the kingdom of God could look like amongst the rich diversity of contributors to the body of Christ:

> Let me develop a quantum interpretation as to why participation is such an effective organizational strategy. In the traditional model, we leave the interpretation of information to senior or expert people. Although they may be aware, to some extent, that

they are interpreting the data, choosing some aspects of it, and ignoring others, few have been aware of how much potential data they lose through acts of observation. A few people, charged with interpreting the data, arc, in fact, observing only very few of the potentialities contained within that data.[229]

Wheatley continues to describe how organisational data can be imagined as a wave moving through time and space; as it moves, it develops more potential explanations. If it only meets one observer, then all that potentiality for interpretation is collapsed into just one interpretation as it is filtered through the expectations and limitations of that singular observer. All the other potential interpretations remain undiscovered and the single interpretation is then passed on as the one interpretation that the organisation as a whole works with. This singular interpretation is often presented as the objective outcome which, of course, it is not, and in some ways complete, which again is a long way from the reality if we take into account all the lost possibilities. Wheatley outlines how we can see this process change if we have a different perspective.

Consider how different it is, in quantum terms, when the wave of information spreads out broadly everywhere in the organization. Instead of 'collapsing' into just a few interpretations, many moments of meeting – hundreds, even thousands of them – will occur. At each of those intersections between an observer and the data, an interpretation will appear, one that is specific to that act of observation. Instead of losing so many of the potentialities contained with the data wave, the multiplicity of interactions can elicit many of those potentials, giving a genuine richness to the data that is lost when we restrict information access to only a few people. An organization swimming in many interpretations can

229. Margaret Wheatley, *Leadership and the New Science: Discovering Order in a Chaotic World* (Oakland, CA: Berrett-Koehler Publishers, 1994), p. 64.

then discuss, combine, and build on them. The outcome of such a process has to be a much more diverse and richer sense of what is going on and what needs to be done.

It would seem that the more participants we engage in this participative universe, the more we can access its potentials and the wiser we can become.[230]

I find Wheatley's approach so inspiring as it expands the possibilities and opportunities that a community can explore together and certainly increases the value of the contributions that all the individuals make in what she calls 'interpreting the data'.

This is a shift from a more Newtonian worldview of laws and functions to a quantum perspective of self-organisation, where relationships matter and everything is seen as a whole rather than individual parts. This is often referred to as 'chaos theory' and is yet another factor under the surface of the changing worldview we are working with in the UK. This helps us as we think about shame-resilient communities, as it encourages greater opportunities for participation and relationship.

---

230. Ibid., p. 65.

Chapter 27: Spurring One Another On

We all know how it feels to be talked over, or told to be quiet. Our feelings of inadequacy and rejection rise up. Having a voice is important, it allows us to put into words our thoughts and ideas and have them shaped by others as they do the same. In this way, we are validated and given a sense of value and place in the world. These are key elements in building our identity and self-worth. It is this relational connection and validation that shame seeks to destroy. This is as true in the lives of our Christian communities as in other areas, especially when it comes to us exploring ideas and thoughts about God and his world.

It has always intrigued me as to why there is such limited space to hear from each other in our gatherings as Christians. It's as if real life and our experiences of God don't matter; they are somehow second rate compared to what the preacher may have prepared. This is particularly strange when we consider that a majority of the Bible is made up of exactly that: ordinary people's experiences of God in their lives. Doesn't this at least give us a case for finding a regular space to hear how we are experiencing and encountering God day to day, and what this looks like for us now?

This is not to minimise what the Bible has to offer us, or diminish its importance. It is simply to say that perhaps the Bible's biggest message to us is that God meets us in every area of our lives, and encourages us to share with each other – and those we spend time with at work, at home, or in our local communities – what this looks like. In this way, once again we are providing an opportunity for shame to be banished as we acknowledge that God meets us in the everyday situations of life, and in doing so empathises with us; he understands and participates in the whole of life with us. 'Let us consider how we may spur one another on towards love and good deeds, not giving up meeting together, as some are in the habit of doing, but encouraging one another – and all the more as you see the Day approaching.'[231]

To 'spur' one another on is an interesting phrase. We spur into action or activity. In this respect, I think genuine encouragement should have an outworking that leads to some sort of further action. I have been told that I am someone who has the gift of encouragement. A friend described my gift of encouragement once as feeling like being 'poked with a sharp stick'. I quite like this analogy because it suggests that the encouragement is prompting change or action caused by a gentle discomfort to get us moving, to spur us on. Yet again, these verses are an 'everyone' statement, containing the 'one another' words; we might like to ask ourselves when we last encouraged someone and spurred them into 'love and good deeds'.

One way that we 'spur one another on towards love and good deeds' is to share how we have done these things ourselves, not in an arrogant way, trying to upstage others, but as an encouragement that these things are possible, often by just taking a little extra thought or being open to God's prompting.

Making space for these stories takes us back to our earlier thoughts about chaos and order. There is no doubt that not everyone's contribution will be thought through or indeed totally appropriate for a more public setting! So once again, we have to risk a certain amount of potential chaos here. Are we secure enough as leaders and indeed Christian communities to let this happen?

In describing what it might look like to lead on this edge, Jordan Peterson challenges us to

'live properly'.

---

231. Hebrews 10:24-25.

Perhaps if we lived properly, we could withstand the knowledge of our own fragility and mortality, without the sense of aggrieved victimhood that produces, first, resentment, then envy, and then the desire for vengeance and destruction. Perhaps, if we lived properly, we wouldn't have to turn to totalitarian certainty to shield ourselves from the knowledge of our own insufficiency and ignorance. Perhaps we could come to avoid those pathways to Hell – and we have seen in the terrible twentieth century just how real Hell can be.[232]

Do you notice the pathway he highlights here, and the classic patterns that produce shame? First, 'aggrieved victimhood' as we feel judged; this is one of the three contributing factors that enables shame to thrive. Then comes resentment, followed by envy; this envy is often at the root of shame as it produces feelings of inferiority because we perceive we lack what others have. So Jordan's call to 'live properly' is one that challenges us to accept and live in the reality of our own 'fragility and mortality' which then avoids the area of totalitarian certainty that in his view has led us down 'those pathways to Hell … in the … twentieth century'.

Well, this is certainly not a journey for the faint-hearted as we venture out together as followers of Christ in the twenty-first century! What I can tell you, from ten plus years of intentionally opening up this space in our Sunday gatherings, is that I would not go back. I say this not because it has been easy or without its challenges, but because of the richness of the contributions that we have experienced and the increased sense of family that has been enabled as we have heard how God has walked with us.

One of the noticeable outcomes of this open time, usually twenty minutes or so on a Sunday morning, is that it has started to break down the sacred secular divide (SSD) that has been very strong in our Western

---

232. Peterson, *12 Rules for Life: An Antidote to Chaos*, p. xxxiv.

thinking. Mark Greene captures this well as he uses the analogy of a peach and compares it to an orange. The orange is divided into sections, or segments as they are called. A peach, however, has a stone in the centre which is surrounded by a single mass of peach. He writes:

> Life's a peach, not an orange the sacred secular divide is the pervasive belief that life is an orange not a peach, that some segments of our life are really important to God – prayer, church services, church-based activities – but that others aren't – work, school, university, sport, the arts, music, rest, sleep, hobbies. SSD is like a virus. It pervades the church and pretty much everyone I know has had it and is a carrier. I've had it. And I struggle against it all the time.[233]

Ultimately, of course, the fruit of the 'one another's will find their expression in all the places highlighted, namely: work, school, university, sport, the arts, music, rest, sleep, hobbies. As we develop these practices in our Christian communities, we can influence all the other places we spend our time. In this way, we are carriers of the kingdom, bringing kingdom transformation wherever we find ourselves. So, this becomes a two-way flow, stories of God at work finding their way into our Christian communities as they are shared amongst us, and we are equipped through this experience and the outward focus in the body of Christ to bring kingdom transformation in all the places we inhabit outside of our Christian communities.

In terms of our Christian communities, one of the battles we face here is making 'subjective truth' which is being shared in personal stories stand alongside what we tend to think of as in more forensic terms 'objective truth', often described as biblical principles, for instance. This is truth that we objectify by separating ourselves from it. We stand at a distance and discuss it as theory.

---

233. Mark Greene, *The Great Divide: The Biggest Challenge Facing the Church Today* (London: LICC, 2010), p. 10.

This reduction into parts and the proliferation of separations has characterised not just organisations, but everything in the world during the past three hundred years. Knowledge has been broken into disciplines and subjects, engineering became a prized science, and people were fragmented – counselled to use different 'parts' of themselves in different settings.[234]

The problem here is that our relatively recent (just 300 years old) worldview is different to the truth we find in the Bible. We have tried our best to make the Bible fit this objective truth paradigm and reduce it down to principles and factual statements but as I have already said, it was largely written as subjective truth, in that people were telling the stories of their encounter with God. As we make room once again to hear each other's stories as part of our gatherings, we are engaging in the process of bringing things back together, working with a peach and not an orange to use Mark Greene's illustration. In doing this, we honour one another and put value on our experiences and encounters with God in everyday life. We are able to empathise with each other and see how God empathises with us in our encounters with him. This counteracts the shame that we can feel in a less relational environment where everything is broken down into component parts and we see and feel the separation.

A local church leader came to visit us one Sunday morning whilst on their sabbatical. I talked to them over coffee afterwards and they told me that what they had experienced with us as people participated was possible because we had 'exceptional people'. I responded by telling them that I thought every church had 'exceptional people'. Ours are not necessarily any more special than others, they are just given the opportunity to talk about their experiences of life and God. I will qualify that by saying that we may have slightly more mature people because

234. Wheatley, *Leadership and the New Science: Discovering Order in a Chaotic World*, p. 27.

they are given opportunities to share and minister to each other and so grow in their faith; however, I think the raw material of our lives is very similar to others in local Christian communities.

This problem of having a perception that you somehow need a quota of extra gifted people who are in some way 'exceptional' and can therefore participate is not a new challenge. The reformer Martin Luther who re-established the 'priesthood of all believers' faced this challenge. 'In the introduction to his German Mass (1526) Luther wrote: 'I neither can nor may as yet set up such a congregation; for I do not as yet have the people for it.'[235]

This is ultimately about being willing to take a risk and starting to explore what participation can look like. Many in church leadership are extremely risk obverse in this area as we are so locked into the performance dynamic attached to leading meetings. This stance, in my view, limits the development of a real sense of community. This has to be central to our agenda for at least two reasons. Firstly, because we believe in a God who is by his very nature Trinitarian and lives and dwells in community. Secondly, because the need to belong in and be part of a community is the cry from our culture, which is racked with shame and looking for a sense of renewed identity and belonging.

'To achieve genuine community the designated leader must lead and control as little as possible in order to encourage others to lead. In so doing, she or he must often admit weakness and risk the accusation of failing to lead.'[236] I was very relieved to read Peck's words recently, as I have on occasion been told that I need to lead more by taking control of situations, not stepping back so much.

Working with the 'one another's makes our Christian communities more inclusive of every area of our lives because they deal with the nitty

---

235. Stuart & Sian Murray Williams, *Multi-Voiced Church* (Milton Keynes: Authentic Publishing, 2012), p. 149.
236. Peck, *The Different Drum*, p. 164.

gritty of life in relationships, and set the agenda for those relationships in our communities. As I have hinted here, working with the 'one another's raises challenges for the way we think about leadership and what our role is as we lead and create atmospheres where we can experience the outworking of the 'one another' statements that characterise a Christian community. We will return to this area and some of the shifts that I think we need to see happen for this vibrant form of life to exist and have space to develop.

Mark Greene articulates so well how many people in our Christian communities feel about themselves. His thoughts on the sacred secular divide, and how it shapes our thinking, are yet another way in which we are made to feel 'less than' others or excluded from the work of the kingdom.

> The SSD [sacred secular divide] leads us to believe that really holy people become missionaries, moderately holy people become pastors, and people who are not much use to God get a job. Bah humbug. Of course, this is not something that missionaries or pastors themselves believe or would, indeed, ever say; but the reality is that the majority of Christians do have a sense that they are second-class citizens of the kingdom of heaven, and that the 110 waking hours they spend in non-church activities each week are not of any substantial interest to the one who created the world he calls us to steward.[237]

We can see how this exclusion from participation in the spiritual life of our Christian communities in so many ways impacts how we see ourselves. It reinforces the message that there must be 'something wrong with me'; the shame idea is compounded through all these experiences – often not deliberately, it's just the way things have been set up. Well, let's recognise what's going on in these and many other situations like them,

---

237. Greene, *The Great Divide: The Biggest Challenge Facing the Church Today*, p. 11.

and decide that enough is enough! Peterson asks us to walk the line, the 'straight and narrow path' as he calls it, 'between order and chaos'[238]. I would suggest that for many of us our Christian communities verge far more towards order as the centre point, so what might it look like to allow a little more chaos to bring a balance?

238. Peterson, *12 Rules for Life: An Antidote to Chaos*, p. xxxiv.

Chapter 28: Unearthing Creativity

Reflections from the pottery

One of the areas that is shut down by shame is our creativity. To be creative involves great vulnerability as we put so much of ourselves into what we create and then in some way offer it to a watching and often critical world.

> But naked vulnerability is not merely a representation of our having been created to be in relationship. God desires us to live like he lives. Thus, to be created in God's image also refers to us having creative dominion within the world. And to be maximally creative also requires that we are vulnerable.[239]

This takes great courage, a courage that is often displayed when we are young and childlike, but is eroded away as we step into adolescence. Restoring this creativity is part of the healing from shame. It can happen in many ways. What I share here are some insights from the pottery studio that we have as part of Network Church.

There is something intrinsically buried in each of us, it rests in the core of our being. It's our desire to emulate our creator God who makes us in his image. This gift, as it is often called, is just that, a gift given to each of us. It stirs in us if we will let it, if we will receive it as a gift and acknowledge it in our lives. It sets a battleground for many, where the weapons of words spoken over us many years ago have won long-held victories in keeping these treasured gifts buried and moribund.

Ask any class of young children who likes making things, and every hand in the room goes up and the air is filled with anticipation and excitement at the prospect. Ask the same question, however, of a group

---

239. Curt Thompson, *The Soul of Shame* (Downers Grove, IL: IVP, 2015), p122.

of teenagers, let alone adults, and the response is very different! A few sheepish hands may be raised, tentatively, and nervousness and a sense of being found out is in the air. So, something happens to these youngsters as they grow up, they lose their sense of fun and freedom to be creative. Thoughts like 'It's not cool to make things' or an overwhelming sense of possible failure loom large in our minds. Fortunately being cool has never featured on my list of things to be. It would appear, however, that being cool and not being seen to fail features very highly for many, and fitting in is essential, and apparently you don't tend to fit in if you own up to making things or being artistic.

Gill and I became friends working together in a little office for a charity serving churches with training and resources for small groups called Cell UK.[240] Gill regularly stayed after hours to 'do her work' as she had spent much of her day in conversation with others in the building. The atmosphere changed through Gill being there and the sense of community that she helped develop was very noticeable.

In one of our many conversations over a cuppa whilst taking a break from the computer, we discovered that we both had a love of pottery, or ceramics as Gill called it! I had enjoyed throwing pots at school as part of my art timetable. In fact, I threw them as part of my language-learning timetable as well, as I managed to convince the French teacher to let me do European studies and then negotiated with the European studies student teacher to let me go and do pottery instead. As a result, my French is practically non-existent and I know very little about Europe; I can, however, throw a pot! Gill, it turned out, had done a couple of ceramics courses and loved all the history associated with the development of the potteries.

Neither of us had followed this up in any way and we both thought it would be good to rekindle our interest. We looked online, found a 'kick

240. https://celluk.org.uk.

wheel' and with the help of a friend, managed to purchase it. We very excitedly went to pick it up, thinking this would be the beginning of our adventures into pottery. Despite our enthusiasm, the wheel sat in the back of my garage largely untouched; other things always took priority over getting together with Gill to throw a pot or two. This, it seems, is often the case with creative endeavours; we find it difficult, somehow, to prioritise and make space for the things that will give us life, especially the creative. I have come to see that this is often because we do not value ourselves and our well-being enough to give ourselves permission to spend time doing those things that give us life, those things that are often of a more creative nature.

A surprise discovery over the summer stirred our interest once again as Gill announced that she had remembered she had a kiln in her shed. (Doesn't everyone!) Sure enough, this proved to be the case. A friend had bought it for her daughter who had subsequently lost interest in pottery, and it had been given to Gill a few years before. Well, there was nothing to stop us now! Or so you might think, but still we didn't seem to get around to doing anything, and this creative project lived only in our minds. The kiln was rescued from the shed, and stood, yes, you guessed it, next to the wheel in the back of my garage. There they sat, keeping each other company, but dormant, just waiting to be put to use.

A combination of events occurred to unlock our stalemate situation. The first was realising that we needed a designated space to work in. We found this through a dear friend Peter Kinahan in the form of a spare room in an old factory building that, with a clear out and a coat of paint, could be used. This was duly done, and the kiln and the wheel were moved in, ready for action. But still we didn't manage to get there to make anything! There always seemed to be more important things in our diaries.

The second breakthrough came when we did something so simple I am rather embarrassed to mention it, and don't know why we didn't think of it before. Gill suggested that we found a time in our diaries when we could agree to meet in our little pottery room once a week. We settled on Wednesdays at 4 p.m. It wasn't rocket science but it made a huge difference. Once it went in the diary it happened, and the fact that I was expecting Gill to be there and she was expecting me meant that we honoured our commitment to 'one another' (there's that phrase again) and turned up. So, for several years now, unless something very major happens, you can find Gill and I in the pottery at 4 p.m. on a Wednesday!

Things gradually took shape; for the first year or so we didn't have running water, not ideal for a pottery. This changed as I fitted a sink and we had cold water at least. Then luxury arrived as a new tank was put in and hot water was available. Something else happened, by accident really; we found ourselves inviting people to join us. We would have conversations and mention that we had a pottery and watch people become energised as they shared stories of how much they enjoyed making things as a child but hadn't done so for ages. They talked fondly of the dinosaur they made as a six-year-old or the pinch pot they had proudly taken home from infants school. As a result, we had a steady stream of people through the door. Our little room was often buzzing with conversations as people sat and painted spots on a mug or had a go on the wheel with squeals of delight as something took shape or, more often than not, spun off, followed by much laughter.

We began to notice how reluctant some were to come into our little room, loitering on the threshold looking sheepish. On more than one occasion there have been tears as people battle with what wells up inside them as they contemplate giving themselves permission to step inside. It was truly a battleground for many. One lady stood in the doorway and told us she was not creative or in any way artistic as the tears rolled down her cheeks. Gill, in her inimitable way, took her hand and led her in to sit and watch, and have a cuppa, telling her that she could just paint spots on a mug, and so it began. You might say it was a form of therapy or recovery, the tears were dried, the paints came out and an adventure began. A long dormant gift began to surface as this lady became a regular visitor. What she created was truly amazing and she loved doing it, working with different colours, experimenting with patterns, sensing the shape of the pot and producing something that flowed so effortlessly. Before long, pots and assorted glazes were being taken home and would return the following week decorated by the person who, by her own confession just a few weeks before, was 'not artistic or in any way creative'!

'So God created mankind in his own image, in the image of God he created them; male and female he created them.'[241] The dominant word in this verse is 'created'. This should speak to us about what it means to be made in God's image. We are created to be like God, who is creative. So, if we are to represent him, then being creative will be one of the signs of this. That's not to say that we should all become artists; that would be a rather narrow view of creativity, but each of us will have ways in which we connect with and express our creativity. Sir Ken Robinson says: 'I define creativity as the process of having original ideas that have value.'[242] This definition expands the horizon for creativity and hopefully draws us back into the space that many have stepped out of. Either because it was not perceived as cool or they were told they would never get a job doing that, or simply made to look foolish in front of others (creating shame in them) as their creation, usually painting or drawing, didn't meet the teacher's expectations.

Another dynamic here is the realisation that is highlighted by Jordan Peterson in an interview with Marc Mayer, former director and CEO of the National Gallery of Canada, that 'systems do not nurture creativity. Telling people what to do and putting them in boxes is counter

---

241. Genesis 1:27.
242. Ken Robinson, *Out of Our Minds* (Chichester: Wiley, 2011), Kindle edition, location 2228.

productive.'[243] The effect of both our education 'system' and much of church life, which has often adopted a systems approach, is to restrict artistic and creative endeavour. Our experiences at the pottery studio have confirmed this in many cases. We have lost sight of the fact that we are created to be creative. Artists have the capacity to draw us out, to take us beyond ourselves; they set our imaginations and emotions alight. Modernity in particular has been sceptical about both of these areas, wanting us to conform to the system so we can be productive in a manufacturing sense of that word. Whilst there is nothing wrong with this in essence, it has had the effect of shutting down and restricting the inner creativity of so many, with the result that we no longer carry one of the hallmarks of our Christian faith – being created in the image of a creative God. We cannot be fully who God has created us to be unless we tackle this loss.

What this will mean for us in our churches will fill some with horror and others with jubilation. It will be a marmite or peanut butter-type moment for us. This is because there is no real middle ground here. It feels as if we have paid lip service at best since the Reformation to the artistic community, and time has finally run out. To unleash creativity into church life, however, will feel like a complete culture shock to many.

We will need wisdom as leaders to open up and release people into this space, and will have to think carefully how we can protect our more artistic friends from criticism and abuse from those who inhabit a different space.

> The world is basically an explored territory inside an unexplored territory, things you know and things you don't know …The artists like to be right out on the edge, and that's the edge between

---

243. Jordan B. Peterson, *Exploring the Psychology of Creativity*, filmed interview with Marc Meyer, May 2017, https://www.youtube.com/watch?v=KxGPe1jD-qY (accessed 8.12.20).

chaos and order. And they like to expand the dimension of order out into the chaos. And they do that first by transforming perception.[244]

This sounds very much like a description of what discipleship needs to look like, and certainly resonates with the idea of the kingdom coming. In this respect, we would all benefit from developing our artistic and creative energy as we engage not only in mission but also in discipleship. We will need those who are already used to doing this, who already carry and use their creative gift, to help us. I have learned much from walking alongside such people, sometimes running to keep up, and often having to ask them to slow down as they explain what they see. They will want to stretch us and take us beyond where we are, into an expansive kingdom territory that stretches far beyond our sometimes limited imaginations. As such, they can appear disruptive and often hard to understand, so we need as leaders to be intermediaries for them, helping them interpret what they see so we can grasp it and help turn it into some sort of reality.

Making space for the artist's expression in our midst so that we may be stimulated to unlock the creative potential in us, has to be one of the key roles of leadership in the twenty-first-century Church. If ever there was a time when we needed to transform perception and explore new territory, it is now! This will not be an easy ride, though, and will demand courageous leadership on our part. We are often well-established in our systems and patterns of worship, and as a friend said to me a few years ago, 'Some of the things we do in church life have really deep roots which you don't realise until you start trying to dig them up.'

So, how can we embark on this change and bring creativity in? Let me share a couple of thoughts on this that may give some hints around

---

244. Ibid.

what this could look like. I guess you might say that I may have a bit of a head start in this area, as I have a pottery studio and enjoy exploring and experimenting with clay and, indeed, other materials. It is, however, still something that I have to make a conscious effort to keep on my radar as a leader.

The default even for me is often to safety, and keeping people happy by avoiding those things that may not be understood easily and may sometimes be interpreted as completely unhelpful by those who want to protect the status quo. In this respect, you have to build people's trust. The best way to do this, in my experience, is by creating safety. These two things can appear to be in tension. On the one hand, we are wanting to push into chaos and explore new things, and on the other hand, we are wanting to do it in a safe way. The tension is very real. One way we create safety is through good explanation; if people have a clear understanding of what is going on and what may be expected of them, then they feel much safer than just being launched into an experience without this explanation. This explanation also needs to continue as the process unfolds, so pausing and explaining is essential. What also helps here is giving space for reflection after the event so we can hear from each other and reflect on what has happened.

Secondly, I have found it helpful to create an atmosphere where this is just for fun! To set the context of play can also be releasing. Once again, this pushes against the performance mentality that can be unhelpfully dominant on occasions. It is rather sad to reflect that much of church life is in the deadly serious box and too often fun can be off the agenda. One way of achieving this playful dimension is to involve children. You can get away with a huge amount if you do it for the benefit of the children and ask the adults to join in, knowing all along, it's the adults that you are really wanting to stretch. Children bring a natural uninhibited playfulness that is contagious, so why not let them lead the way and ride on their enthusiasm? I love the title of a TED Talk given by Charlie Mackesy: 'Abandon the Idea of Being Good and Just Try'.[245]

Chapter 30 highlights a few things we have explored together at Network Church in this respect. These have been over a period of time, and as you will see, have often started with a spark and grown. The ideas have been stimulated by a particular individual's passions or insights. In this respect, our role as leaders has not been so much to come up with a detailed plan but to map out the sort of spaces we want to create for all of us to engage in together, and fan into flame those things that God reveals. The so-called lack of vision that is created in this approach has been an issue for some who want to know more specifically our tangible goals and aims for the coming year and be told exactly what to do! In an attempt to put some description around the core things that I thought were central to us, I came up with eight headings and pictures that were an attempt to describe the sort of vision I had for us as a community. So, before we look at a few specific examples of what we have experimented with, here are the eight snapshots I came up with.

---

245. Charlie Mackesy, TED Talk, 'Abandon the Idea of Being Good and Just Try', September 2018, https://www.ted.com/talks/charlie_mackesy_abandon_the_idea_of_being_good_and_just_try (accessed 8.12.20).

Chapter 29: Signposts

In an attempt to summarise how the 'one another' statements were being outworked in and through our Christian community at Network Church, I put together the following words and pictures. They provide signposts about where we are heading together, as well as reminders of some of our shared beliefs and values. They act in part to form a description of the atmospheres we are creating together as we seek to be a shame-resilient community. You will see a number of the areas we have looked at echoed in these eight statements and descriptions.

They are deliberately short and as ever, the pictures seemed to communicate more than the words. They sit under eight headings as follows:

Reversing the gravitational pull of Church

This is about a 'go' rather than 'come' mentality. Isn't it interesting that Jesus sends the disciples out and says he will be with them as they go?

Then Jesus came to them and said, 'All authority in heaven and on earth has been given to me. Therefore go and make disciples of all nations, baptising them in the name of the Father and of the Son and of the Holy Spirit, and teaching them to obey everything I have commanded you. And surely I am with you always, to the very end of the age.'[246]

---

246. Matthew 28:18-20.

Often we are trying to pull people in. It's about being out in the world and how we live 24/7. The kingdom is compared to yeast: 'The kingdom of heaven is like yeast that a woman took and mixed into about thirty kilograms of flour until it worked all through the dough.'[247] What a fantastic picture of the transforming nature of the kingdom in the world.

The People Revolution

The Reformation was about the 'priesthood of all believers'. Bill Beckham states that what we are experiencing now is the second Reformation which is the outworking of this belief in practice as we encourage 'every member ministry'.[248] The amazing fact of the gospel is that Jesus through His Spirit lives in us.

And I will ask the Father, and he will give you another advocate to help you and be with you for ever – the Spirit of truth.

The world cannot accept him, because it neither sees him nor knows him. But you know him, for he lives with you and will be in you.[249]

This means that each one of us is empowered by the Holy Spirit and called to the work of the kingdom, and not just a special few.

---

247. Matthew 13:33.
248. William A. Beckham, *The Second Reformation* (Houston, TX: Touch, 1995).
249. John 14:16-17.

Working around centres of energy

 Christianity spread through the known world of the first century at some speed. It was mobile in nature, and was contained and carried in the lives of individual believers and vibrant small communities. We catch glimpses of these through the New Testament writings. 1 Corinthians comments on the church that met at the home of Aquila and Priscilla.

> The churches in the province of Asia send you greetings. Aquila and Priscilla greet you warmly in the Lord, and so does the church that meets at their house.[250]

This was one of the many centres of spiritual energy that developed and multiplied. We likewise need to be recognising and encouraging these spiritual centres of energy and giving them freedom to develop and grow.

Having permeable edges

 Jesus spends quite a bit of his time hanging around with people, often people who were thought to be unsuitable to be engaging with. We see a lovely response to this in Matthew's Gospel where Jesus eats with tax collectors and sinners.

---

250. 1 Corinthians 16:19.

While Jesus was having dinner at Matthew's house, many tax collectors and sinners came and ate with him and his disciples. When the Pharisees saw this, they asked his disciples, 'Why does your teacher eat with tax collectors and sinners?'[251]

They felt at home with him as he extended friendship to them. So we need to be 'open-handed' with our gatherings and make them accessible. This is particularly true, as people want to belong before they believe.

Cultivating an earthed spirituality that is Jesus-focused

I have found it interesting to reflect on how much of church life has been centred on Old Testament ideas and how much is informed by the New Testament. Now, before anyone gets uptight, we believe in the whole canon of Scripture from Genesis to Revelation. However, we are called to follow Jesus, and to live informed by his teachings and example.

I find it fascinating that artists down the centuries have painted Jesus as a rather ethereal character in neatly pressed white robes with the all-too familiar halo. Whilst I can understand why this has been done, I think the Jesus we follow is a far more earthy character and calls us to live in vibrant connectivity with our world; the sort of Jesus that would light a fire and cook breakfast on the beach with his friends.[252]

---

251. Matthew 9:10-11.
252. John 21:1-14.

Nurturing authentic friendships and healthy community

Jesus calls us his friends.

I no longer call you servants, because a servant does not know his master's business. Instead, I have called you friends, for everything that I learned from my Father I have made known to you.[253]

So, from the basis of our friendship with Jesus, we create friendship with others. Authentic friendships are those that are committed to the friendship without presupposed outcomes. They are also friendships that engage and deal with the real issues of life. From this foundation, healthy communities can be formed and flourish.

Holding deep convictions but being unfazed by questions

Our beliefs as Christians are distinct, and form the basis for our values and actions that flow from them. For others to understand this link between beliefs values and actions, I think we need to engage more in questions. Dare I suggest, invite questions around what we believe and why? Jesus invited and asked questions all the time.

'But what about you?' he asked. 'Who do you say I am?' Simon Peter answered, 'You are the Messiah, the Son of the living God.'[254]

Jesus asks many questions, for instance, 'Who do you say I am?' These

253. John 15:15.
254. Matthew 16:15-16.

questions engage him in healthy dialogue with people around issues of faith. Let's become like Jesus and ask good questions.

Stimulating faith development through participation at every stage of the journey

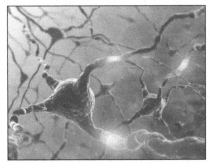

The idea of life-long learning has become increasingly popular. As Christians we have, however, gone for the more knowledge-based learning style rather than the apprentice model that is more closely linked to discipleship that involves the whole of our lives. It is interesting that Romans 12 starts with our bodies and then moves to our minds:

> Therefore, I urge you, brothers and sisters, in view of God's mercy, to offer your bodies as a living sacrifice, holy and pleasing to God – this is your true and proper worship. Do not conform to the pattern of this world, but be transformed by the renewing of your mind. Then you will be able to test and approve what God's will is – his good, pleasing and perfect will.[255]

255. Romans 12:1-2.

Chapter 30: Playful Spaces

Playful spaces connect back into our earlier thoughts about creativity. Having atmospheres that feel play-like encourage creativity and give those involved permission and safety to have a go at exploring something with others. It is when we are at play that we find out who we are and interact with others and form relationships and bonds. We have an opportunity to reveal areas of our inner world that others may not realise exist; this, in turn, helps us to put words and actions around these. All of this helps us to build a picture of who we are in association with those we are at play with. The same can be true for us in our Christian communities as we learn to engage together in meaningful ways. One of the ways we can do this is through what I think of as playful spaces, 'just for fun' times, as I sometimes describe them. Here are some examples of the sort of things we have tried together. These examples have happened over a period of time and many of them were before the Covid restrictions, which meant we had to think through how we worked within the guidelines during the pandemic. Many of the ideas are now being reintroduced as Covid subsides.

Drawing boards

For a number of years now, we have had a large drawing board as part of our Sunday services. It started as a place where one of our artists could draw. This particular artist liked drawing large-scale with charcoal, so I purchased two internal household doors, and made a frame so they could stand together and be supported safely. As we were renting a building for our Sunday gatherings, they had to come apart and be able to be stored away; this has proved useful in other respects, as it means they can be transported and set up in other places as well. This drawing board idea began as an experiment, a trial just to see how it would work.

Needless to say, as with many things temporary, the boards have been modified and changed, adding an additional board, so there are now three and they have continued to be used for a number of years now. These modifications mean that the total drawing surface is now 2.4m wide by 2m high. The boards are covered in lining paper of a reasonable thickness, which is fixed on each week with masking tape. We soon discovered that the charcoal makes a bit of a mess so we put one of those easy-wipe plastic tablecloths in front of the board to save cleaning the floor every week.

I had envisioned these drawing boards becoming a regular part of our gathering, but soon discovered that not everyone thought they should be. There was no malice here, just some resistance to putting them up, and in particular, fitting the paper. This seemed to press a number of people's buttons. I thought perhaps they might have had some disastrous experiences hanging wallpaper or something similar in the past, which was putting them off! What I discovered on reflection was that it wasn't that simple. What was going on here was a values issue. Yes, it was a bit of effort to put up the board and add the paper, but nothing compared to getting the chairs out or setting up the PA. These other areas were seen as essential, whereas the art board was not; it was optional in people's minds. There needed to be a values shift and I needed to head the charge. It would have been sacrilege to not have singing as part of our worship or not have a sermon of some sort. I wanted the art space to be in this same league and have the same value attached to it. What this meant was taking leadership in this area, which involved encouraging it to be set up – setting it up myself if no one else did, and making sure that the chalks and charcoal were put out ready to be used, as they often were left in the box, which in my mind was like turning up to lead sung worship and leaving your guitar in its case! I had all sorts of excuses along the way and still do at times, from 'I am not sure we have anyone who wants to draw this morning' to 'so and so who usually draws is away so it's not worth putting it up'. On a few occasions no one has drawn or written on it but over fifteen years or so, I can count those occasions on one hand.

Initially the board was used to illustrate the talks to great effect. Cartoon-like characters in their settings punctuated with words as prompts and reminders filled the board. Many of our speakers wondered what everyone was laughing at, and it was only as they turned to see the drawings that they realised what was coming to life over their left shoulder on the boards as they spoke. The impact of this was really seen in our midweek small groups where people remembered the drawings and were able to recall the talk through these illustrations in a way that they could not have done without them. This was particularly useful as the groups used the Sunday material for their study and application each week, challenging each other as to how what had been taught would make a difference to their lives.

The boards morphed over time into a place that is used during the sung worship time and often depicts a life-size picture which picks up on the theme of the service. It has also led to prophetic words being given through what has been drawn, as someone in the congregation steps forward to share what God has revealed through the picture to them. It has been a great space for the children of all ages to express their worship. It is particularly chaotic and somewhat magical to see a mixture of adults and children all gathered round it, creating a masterpiece together. In this respect, it's just for fun and is a non-judgemental space where anyone can pitch in and make a contribution. This attitude also takes it out of the 'performance space' and avoids judgement on anyone's doodles. This, of course, is key if we are going to release people from any shame that they may carry around this area.

The boards have also created a space to write as well as draw. Sometimes it's just a phrase or a few words that someone has carried in their heart for the last week and would not want to speak it out, but are able to write it on the board so it can be included as part of our worship. As you can imagine, scriptures get written up and often pre-empt what the person speaking that morning has prepared.

Creating interactive experiences

Often our Bibles can stay as two-dimensional places as words on a page; it is helpful to bring the stories to life by making them a three-dimensional experience. Using props and engaging those present in the stories is one way of doing this effectively.

With this in mind, I built a boat. It all slots and ties together with rope, having a mast and sail and being big enough for two or three people to climb in and sit on board. There are a number of Bible stories that involve boats, and it has been used quite a bit in all sorts of ways. The first task is to put it together, which can involve a number of volunteers. Whilst this is happening, you can set the scene for the story and then invite people to come and play the parts of the characters in the story and climb in the boat as required.

What has been fascinating has been to ask the individuals involved to share what it is like to be immersed in the story and share their observations and insights. We typically spend a lot of time in our heads trying to understand things. So, to get us into our bodies experiencing the things we are trying to understand and allowing our hearts to connect as we do, can be very powerful.

Other ways this has happened include:

A biblical bush tucker trial. Like the kind run in the popular television series *I'm a Celebrity ... Get Me Out of Here!* The service was being led by some of the young people in the church, ably supported by their parents. They asked for two volunteers and two of our chaps stepped forward. They were blindfolded as contestants and were given food found in the Bible and had to guess what it was. The church was divided in two, and scored a point for their side if they could find the Bible reference for the food. As you can imagine, we had great fun with locusts, figs and Whatsits, more commonly known as manna! I will let you try to work out the connection here.

Using the potter's wheel. Giving out clay as I throw something on the wheel has been another way to engage beyond our heads with a topic or story. It is amazing what people mould their clay into in just a few moments, and it is great to share our creations with each other afterwards and see what people have made. There is something magical about watching someone throw on a wheel and I often tell the familiar Bible stories of Jeremiah at the potter's house[256] or us being jars of clay from second Corinthians.[257]

These are just a couple of examples of the more playful spaces that we have tried to create together, so we can learn in a different way. These sorts of adventures have the spin-offs of building relationships as well as allowing creativity to happen, often spontaneously, amongst us. What occurs on these occasions can be quite profound and leaves a lasting legacy in people's hearts and minds. It is a great way to encourage the 'one another's as we often all end up getting involved. My hope is that the level of participation engagement and therefore inclusion all help to make these environments shame-resilient, and are places where our gifts and contributions can be valued and we can find our place in an accepting Christian family.

---

256. Jeremiah 18:1-11.
257. 2 Corinthians 4:1-12.

Chapter 31: Equipping the Saints for the Work of Ministry

Using a different lens: an Ephesians 4 Bible study

As I mentioned earlier, one of the drivers in our guilt-innocence framework has been to get things right to avoid 'wrongdoing'. From this premise, it should come as no surprise that we have organised our structures around this idea. This has been good for us in some areas, but has caused problems in others. When it comes to looking through the lens of shame rather than guilt, however, we need to start from a different place. Our starting place is the 'something wrong with me' assumption rather than 'I have done something wrong'.

Creating places where people can be affirmed as valuable and included becomes a core part of the salvation process. With this in mind, our Christian communities face the challenge of becoming these sorts of places. This will mean we will have to rethink some of our old ways of working and embrace a more inclusive and less judgemental stance. This will bring with it the need to re-interpret some of our well-known biblical passages as we look at them through a different lens. One of the ways we will need to do this is by changing our more individualistic and often hierarchical approach to have a more community or relational hermeneutic. I think a good example of this can be found in part of Ephesians 4, entitled 'Unity and maturity in the body of Christ'. As you will see, this passage contains a further 'one another' statement: 'bearing with one another in love'.[258]

We will once again look at the role that leadership has occupied and the shifts that need to take place in this area as we move forward. As I have said already, we have often thought of the ministry being done

---

258. Ephesians 4:2.

by leaders, as they have dominated this place in many of our churches. Unknowingly we have often translated this into how we then read our Bibles. Where something spiritual is initiated or is outworked, we see it through this lens of leadership; in doing this, we can count ourselves out of being involved if we are not a leader, as the spiritual work is typically done by the leaders. After all, we tell ourselves, they have the training, they are the 'special people' who know what to do and how to do it when it comes to spiritual things. As the so-called 'laity', we are the receivers rather than the delivers of ministry, and in this respect can become passive and lose our sense of value to ourselves, others and God. It is commonly understood that the laity are normal people and the clergy are special or professional; we often use the words 'priest' and 'minister' to describe them. This keeps us as 'the laity' in the shame space, believing there is 'something wrong with us', which excludes us from participating in the spiritual life of this community and also separating us from the God who wants to work through us. We will see how this plays out as we look at Ephesians 4 in a moment.

It is also interesting to note that it is as Jesus 'ascended on high' that 'he took many captives and gave gifts to his people'.[259] This, of course, references back to our earlier thoughts on the place of the ascension in our gospel message and its implications for us as we are empowered by the Holy Spirit to bring God's gifts to his body and the world at large. In so doing, Jesus includes us in his purposes as we take up our place in his body and become more fully the people he created us to be. As we take up our place, the shame that we carry continues to be redeemed; we are included, we are valued, given a voice and accepted. Indeed, we could say that what is taken captive in this context is our lack of value and being seen as unworthy, which is demonstrated in our feelings of shame.

Many of these ideas have been just that for us, and kept in the 'ideas only' category; things that we know as knowledge but have not seen

---

259. Ephesians 4:8.

outworked in our experience as they would have been in the context in which they were originally created. They were delivered originally by way of instructions to help these vibrant, early Christian communities thrive and flourish through practical hands-on experience.

Enough preamble, let's look at the passage in question. I have included it here so you can read it, and together we can look to see how these words can speak to us in our current context today.

Unity in the Body of Christ

I therefore, the prisoner in the Lord, beg you to lead a life worthy of the calling to which you have been called, with all humility and gentleness, with patience, bearing with one another in love, making every effort to maintain the unity of the Spirit in the bond of peace. There is one body and one Spirit, just as you were called to the one hope of your calling, one Lord, one faith, one baptism, one God and Father of all, who is above all and through all and in all.

But each of us was given grace according to the measure of Christ's gift. Therefore it is said,

'When he ascended on high he made captivity itself a captive; he gave gifts to his people.'

(When it says, 'He ascended,' what does it mean but that he had also descended into the lower parts of the earth? He who descended is the same one who ascended far above all the heavens, so that he might fill all things.) The gifts he gave were that some would be apostles, some prophets, some evangelists, some pastors and teachers, to equip the saints for the work of ministry, for building up the body of Christ, until all of us come to the unity of the faith and of the knowledge of the Son of God, to maturity, to the measure of the full stature of Christ. We must no longer be children, tossed to and fro and blown about by every wind of doctrine, by people's trickery, by their craftiness in deceitful scheming. But speaking the truth in love, we must grow up in every way into him who is the head, into Christ, from whom the whole body, joined and knit together by every ligament with which it is equipped, as each part is working properly, promotes the body's growth in building itself up in love.[260]

The gifts described here of apostle, prophet, evangelist, pastor and teacher are often quoted as being the five-fold gifts of leadership. You therefore sometimes hear conversations about leadership teams needing to have all five of these gifts represented on the team by different individuals. Some say that an apostle, who is often seen in this context as the main leader in these situations, should carry all the other four gifts, which is what sets him (and it usually is a him in these situations) apart as the apostle. These type of settings tend to be hierarchical in nature. The mention of Christ as the head of the body (v. 15) seems to get overlooked in any practical sense.

This shows how leader-centric we have become in the body of Christ. The setting and context of these five gifts in this passage is not, in my view, about leadership at all, but body life. We can see this by looking at the opening verses; 'bearing with one another', in verse 2, for instance, is body language and is one of the fifty-eight 'one another' phrases of the New Testament which are the descriptions of body life and encouragements for it to be upheld and continued. More explicitly in verse 4 we see the phrase 'There is one body', hence my insistence that this is about the body as a whole and not leadership. If this was not enough, we see in verse 7 the phrase, 'But to each one of us grace has been given as Christ apportioned it.' So just to be clear, these five gifts are given by Christ to each of us, not just those who are leaders.

---

260. Ephesians 4:1-16, NRSV.

This passage is about 'each one of us', not just a few of us. Therefore, when in verse 11 Paul talks about the five-fold gifts Jesus gave, this is the specific outworking of verse 7 and so needs to be understood in terms of 'each one of us'. Just to bring it home one final time, verse 8 says, 'When he ascended on high, he took many captives and gave gifts to his people.' 'His people' here suggests all of his people, not just some of them. This, in my view, should lead us to think very differently, both about the nature of these gifts as well as how and where they are used.

Let's take a step back for a moment and take a purely mathematical approach to a hypothetical group of say 100 people in a Christian community, just for the sake of convenience.

If we apply the five-fold gifts to the body of 100 members, rather than to a small leadership group, and if these five gifts are given equally, then that would mean that twenty people could be apostolic, twenty pastoral, and so on. Before you get too uptight about the numbers, I am not suggesting that we have equal numbers of each gift. However, it would be quite likely that there would be a reasonable spread of the five gifts mentioned here across any group of 100 Christians.

Now, you may say, 'Well, that might be all very well, but on who and where are the 100 Christians going to use their gifts?' If these gifts are simply for leadership, then leaders could use them for the benefit of everyone else, i.e. those who are not leaders. As a good starting place, I think everyone should be using their gifts for the benefit of everyone else in the body. This is made explicit by verse 16, 'From him the whole body, joined and held together by every supporting ligament, grows and builds itself up in love, as each part does its work.'

So, let's make it practical. Those who show a dominant pastoral gift should equip others to be more pastoral and thereby 'equip his people for works of service' (v. 12). I for one would like to see some prophetic people have their latent pastoral gift encouraged and developed, as in my view they as prophets are sometimes not the most pastorally sensitive. Similarly, those with an evangelistic gift would help each of us to share our faith more effectively and so on.

In this way the whole body would work together just as the passage suggests, and the whole body would be built up as 'each part does its work' (v. 16) and all of us could 'become mature, attaining to the whole measure of the fullness of Christ' (v. 13). In this way, the whole body would be 'joined and held together' in the way Paul describes (v. 16).

You might then ask: what is the role of leadership in this scenario?

Well, each of us will firstly be doing what everyone else is doing and using our main gift to build up the body. We will also, along with everyone else, be receiving from others, so we can be built up and be part of the body and grow in maturity. As leaders, our role is to make sure that all the above is given space and encouraged to happen. This means that we will need to be intentional about giving time and space for body ministry where the 'one another's can be worked out. Making space for the prophetic voices to be heard, creating opportunities for those with a teaching gift to teach, and so on. If this was taken seriously, I believe it would radically change the way we both understand each other and the part each of us play in the body. It would shape and radically change how we spend our time and what we do when we come together.

As far as shame is concerned, I think the empathetic atmosphere created as we all respond to each other could be very healing. The role of leadership would be key here, as an atmosphere of acceptance needs to be maintained and opportunities for clarification, understanding and openness need to be created. These are skills that leaders will need to develop, to help these environments flourish. Something we haven't mentioned yet is the need we will have to 'forgive one another if any of you has a grievance against someone'[261] There is that 'one another'

---

261. Colossians 3:13.

phrase again! We can be sure that as each of us practise our gifts there will be things that do not go as well as they should, and we will need to establish good patterns of ensuring that our relationships develop and forgiveness can flow where it needs to.

This is a big ask as it means we as leaders will have to trust that people will step into the arena. We will need to be open to others using their gifts and sometimes messing up along with us as we experiment together so we can all learn. This will not happen overnight, as many members in the body have remained underdeveloped and have not been given space or encouragement to use their gifts. There will be some pain and heartache on the way. Some will be reluctant because they have stepped out before and been hurt by the experience, so acceptance humility and encouragement will need to be among our top values.

Reflecting on the idea of how a community can participate together effectively, Scott Peck suggests the following:

> When I am the designated leader I have found that once a group becomes a community, my nominal job is over. I can sit back and relax and be one among many, for another of the essential characteristics of community is a total decentralisation of authority. Remember that it is antitotalitarian. Its decisions are reached by consensus. Communities have sometimes been referred to as leaderless groups. It is more accurate, however, to say that a community is a group of all leaders.[262]

I have certainly found this to be true on a number of occasions as the community of Network Church has developed.

The sense of acceptance and appreciation of the gifts across the body of Christ and the space to practise using them will, in my view, go a long way to developing more relationally connected Christian communities.

---

262. Peck, *The Different Drum*, p. 72.

A result of this is that they will become more shame resilient. In this way, we will counteract the shame that so many feel as we share together. The sense of being responsible to and for one another that develops out of this scenario will be immense. People will feel empowered and have the thrill of seeing others grow as well, as we all minister to each other. In this way, our ties together will be strengthened and we would, as Ephesians 4:2 says, 'Be completely humble and gentle; be patient, bearing with one another in love' as we 'Make every effort to keep the unity of the Spirit through the bond of peace'.

> Because it is a safe place, compulsive leaders feel free in community – often for the first time in their lives – to *not* lead. And the customary shy and reserved feel free to step forth with their latent gifts of leadership. The result is that a community is an ideal decision-making body. The expression 'A camel is a horse created by a committee' does not mean that group decisions are inevitably clumsy and imperfect; it does mean that committees are virtually never communities.[263]

Another dimension here, of course, is that all this is done because the body of Christ has a purpose beyond itself. Jesus came to bring in the kingdom – it is this kingdom that he constantly talks about. If we are really his body, then we need to be about his business and be involved in seeing the kingdom come. Whilst we have focused on the internal workings of the body as they are described in the passage here, this will inevitably spill out into all the areas of our lives. What I mean by this is that as we find our feet and make our contribution as a member of the body of Christ, so we will have the confidence to do that in our family, workplace and local community. All the time we remain undeveloped within the body of Christ, we also restrict who we are becoming beyond it.

---

263. Ibid.

Imagine the transformation in other situations if the internal workings of the body of Christ described here were applied, where appropriate, to our workplaces!

In conclusion

My hope is that your heart has been stirred and your thinking challenged and extended as you have read these pages. I think that the opportunities that present themselves offer us exciting possibilities for new ways to share the gospel with our friends. We are also presented with many challenges around how we shape ourselves as Christian communities. Let us not shrink back but grasp the things that have struck a chord with us, and press on. You might like to start a reading group and talk to others about what has been highlighted for you in these pages; wrestle together with the concepts, praying that God will lead and inspire you.

I pray that God will give you fresh insights into how you can effectively share the timeless message of Jesus in a way that speaks to those who carry shame; that also you will be able to notice shame in your own life and those of others who are not aware of it and be drawn, and draw others, to a God who empathises and carries our shame, offering us a new start by renewing our whole being – who empowers us to live for him by sending his Holy Spirit to indwell us and in so doing, re-values us and enables us to live life to the full.

I pray that you will find your true personhood in the God who calls you by name, breathes his life into you and simply asks that you become fully who he has created you to be, sharing this newly found life with others who have done the same, so we can represent him as those who carry his image and engage in seeing his kingdom come in our world. May we learn to take his presence into every area of our lives: school, college, workplace, family and neighbourhood.

Bibliography

Barna Group, 'Talking Jesus', research carried out by the Barna Group on behalf of the Church of England, Evangelical Alliance and HOPE, 2015, https://talkingjesus.org/wp-content/uploads/2018/04/Talking-Jesus.pdf

Barrow, Simon & Bartley Jonathan, eds, *Consuming Passion: Why the Killing of Jesus Really Matters* (London: Darton, Longman & Todd, 2005)

Baum, David, 'The Power of Walking Conversations', https://www.davidbaum.com/news/2018/2/4/the-power-of-walking-conversations

Beckham, William A., *Redefining Revival* (Houston, TX: Touch Outreach Ministries, 2001)

Bell, Rob, *Dust*, Nooma DVD (Grand Rapids, MI: Flanel, 2005), https://www.youtube.com/watch?v=kM3qHBAekhg

Benedict, Ruth, *The Chrysanthemum and the Sword*, short review, 8 June 2015, https://jpninfo.com/10394

Berger, Peter, *The Sacred Canopy* (New York, NY: Anchor Books, 1990)

Boyd, Gregory A., 'Atonement: What is the Christus Victor View?', https://reknew.org/2019/01/atonement-what-is-the-christus-victor-view

Boyd, Gregory A., *Cross Vision* (Minneapolis, MN: Fortress Press, 2018)

Boys, Gregory A., *God at War: The Bible & Spiritual Conflict* (Westmont, IL: IVP, 1997).

Boyd, Gregory A., *Satan and the Problem of Evil: Constructing a Trinitarian Warfare Theodicy* (Downers Grove, IL: IVP, 2001)

Boyd, Gregory A., 'The "Christus Victor" View of the Atonement', https://reknew.org/2018/11/the-christus-victor-view-of-the-atonement/

Boyd, Gregory A. & Paul R. Eddy, *Across the Spectrum: Understanding Issues in Evangelical Theology* (Ada, MI: Baker Academic, 2002)

Brown, Brené, Appendix to *Daring Greatly*, https://brenebrown.com/the-research

Brown, Brené, *Dare to Lead: Brave Work. Tough Conversations. Whole Hearts* (London: Vermilion, 2018)

Brown, Brené, *Daring Greatly* (London: Penguin Life, 2015)

Brown, Brené, TED Talk, 'Listening to Shame', March 2012, https://www.ted.com/talks/brene_brown_listening_to_shame

Brené Brown, TED Talk, 'Listening to Shame', March 2012, https://www.ted.com/talks/brene_brown_listening_to_shame (accessed 1.12.20); Brené Brown, TED Talk, 'The Power of Vulnerability', June 2010, https://www.ted.com/talks/brene_brown_the_power_of_vulnerability

Burnhope, Steve, *Jesus Saves… But How? Telling the Story of Atonement in Today's World* (A Kingdom Praxis Solo) (North Hollywood, CA: Basileia Publishing: An Imprint of Harmon Press, 2012), Kindle edition.
Butcher, Catherine, *Who Do You Say I Am?* (HOPE & CV, 2017)

Campanale, Andrea, 'A Gospel that Overcomes Shame' in eds Cathy Ross and Colin Smith, *Missional Conversations* (London: SCM Press, 2018),

Campanale, Andrea, eds Jonny Baker and Cathy Ross, *The Pioneer Gift* (Norwich: Canterbury Press, 2014)

Cell UK, www.celluk.org.uk

Comiskey, Joel, *The Spirit-filled Small Group* (Edmond, OK: CCS Publishing, 2013)

Cozens, Simon, *Looking Shame in the Eye* (London: IVP, 2019)

Finney, John. Emerging Evangelism (London: Darton, Longman & Todd, 2004)

Finlan, Stephen, *Problems With Atonement* (Collegeville, MN: Liturgical Press, 2005)

Forster, Roger, *Trinity* (Milton Keynes, Authentic Media, 2004)

Friendship First, http://friendshipfirst.org

Frost, Matthew, 'Setting God's People Free. A Report from the Archbishops' Council' (Renewal and Reform, 2017), https://www.churchofengland.org/sites/default/files/2017-11/gs-2056-setting-gods-people-free.pdf

Frost, Rob, *Essence*, https://ww w.sharejesusinternational.com/essence

Garlington, D.B., *New Dictionary of Christian Ethics and Pastoral Theology* (Leicester: IVP, 1995)

Gempf, Conrad, *Jesus Asked. What He Wanted to Know* (Grand Rapids, MI: Zondervan, 2003)

Gempf, Conrad, *Mealtime Habits of the Messiah* (Grand Rapids, MI: Zondervan, 2005)

George, Carl F., *Prepare Your Church for the Future* (Tarrytown, NY: Revell, 1991),

Georges, Jayson and Mark D. Baker, *Ministering in Honor-Shame Cultures* (Downers Grove, IL: IVP, 2016)

Georges, Jayson, 'Sin and Shame', HonorShame http://honorshame.com/sin-and-shame-relationship

Georges, Jayson, *The 3D Gospel*, http://honorshame.com/wp-content/uploads/2014/10/Theology-Guide-Guilt-Shame-Fear-Georges.pdf

Georges, Jayson, *The 3D Gospel: Ministry in Guilt, Shame, and Fear Cultures* (Tim& 275 Press, 2014)

Greene, Mark, *The Great Divide: The Biggest Challenge Facing the Church Today* (London: LICC, 2010)

Grimsrud, Ted, Online journal, https://peacetheology.files.wordpress.com/2011/10/atla0001746158.pdf

Gumbel, Nicky, *Alpha Manual* (London: Alpha International, 2001; second revised edition)

Hiebert, Paul G., 'Conversion, Culture and Cognitive Categories', Gospel in Context 1 (4):24-29, 1978, https://danutm.files.wordpress.com/2010/06/hiebert-paul-g-conversion-culture-and-cognitive-categories.pdf

Hyde, Eric, 'The Individual and the Church: John Zizioulas and the Eastern Orthodox Perspective', 27 December 2011, https://ehyde.wordpress.com/2011/12/27/the-individual-and-the-church-john-zizioulas-and-the-eastern-orthodox-perspective/

Jersak. Bradley, *A More Christlike God* (Pasadena, CA: Plain Truth Ministries, 2015)

Kreider, Alan, *The Change of Conversion and the Origin of Christendom* (New York: Continuum International Publishing Group – Trinity, 1999)

Lewis, C.S., *Mere Christianity* (London: William Collins, 2016)

Mann, Alan, *Atonement for a 'Sinless' Society* (Milton Keynes: Authentic Media, 2005)

Marshall, H.I., *Jesus the Savior* (Downers Grove, IL: IVP, 1990)

McGilcrest, Ian, *The Master and His Emissary: The Divided Brain and the Making of the Western World* (New Haven, CT, and London: Yale University Press, 2009)

McIntyre, John, *The Shape of Soteriology: Studies in the Doctrine of the Death of Christ* (London: T&T Clarke, 1995)

Merton, Thomas, *New Seeds of Contemplation* (London: Hollis & Carter, 1949)

Murray Williams, Stuart & Sian, *Multi-Voiced Church* (Milton Keynes: Authentic Publishing, 2012)

Murray, Stuart, *Church After Christendom* (Milton Keynes: Paternoster Press, 2004)

Network Church, https://www.networkchurch.org

Pattison, Stephen, *Shame: Theory, Therapy, Theology* (Cambridge: Cambridge University Press, 2008)

Peck, M. Scott, *The Different Drum* (London: Arrow Books, 1990)

Peck, M. Scott, *The Road Less Travelled* (London: Arrow Books, 1990)

Peterson, Jordan B., *12 Rules For Life: An Antidote to Chaos* (London: Penguin, 2019)

Peterson, Jordan B., filmed interview with Marc Meyer, May 2017, https://www.youtube.com/watch?v=KxGPe1jD-qY

Rohr, Richard, *The Universal Christ: How a Forgotten Reality Can Change Everything We See, Hope For and Believe* (London: SPCK, 2019)

Robinson, Ken, TED Talk, 'Do Schools Kill Creativity?', 2006, https://www.ted.com/talks/ken_robinson_says_schools_kill_creativity/transcript#t-23

Robinson, Ken, *Out of Our Minds: Learning to Be Creative* (Mankato, MN: Capstone Publishing, 2011)

Singlehurst, Laurence, *The Gospel Message Today* (Cambridge: Grove Books, 2013)

Singlehurst, Laurence, *Sowing Reaping Keeping* (Nottingham: IVP, 2006).

Spencer, Nick, *Beyond Belief?: Barriers and Bridges to Faith Today* (London: LICC, 2004)

Stibbe, Mark, *Home at Last* (Milton Keynes: Malcolm Down Publishing, 2017)

The Transforming Shame Network, a community of faith willing and wanting to share human experience, ministerial praxis, academic research and creativity with the hope of transforming shame within church and culture. https://www.transformingshame.co.uk/

Thompson, Curt, *The Soul of Shame* (Downers Grove, IL: IVP, 2015)

Tilby, Angela, *The Seven Deadly Sins: Their Origin in the Spiritual Teaching of Evagrius the Hermit* (London: SPCK, 2009)

Urban, Tim, 'Why Generation Y Yuppies Are Unhappy', 9 September 2013, https://waitbutwhy.com/2013/09/why-generation-y-yuppies-are-unhappy.html

Weaver, J. Denny, *The Nonviolent Atonement* (Grand Rapids, MI: Eerdmans Publishing, 2001; second edition)

Wheatley, Margaret, *Leadership and the New Science: Discovering Order in a Chaotic World* (Oakland, CA: Berrett-Koehler Publishers, 1994)

Wilson, Andrew, 'Jesus' Divine Self-Consciousness', 2014, https://thinktheology.co.uk/blog/article/bntc_2014_jesus_divine_self_consciousnessAngela

Wimber, John, *Everyone Gets to Play* (Garden City, ID: Ampelon Publishing, 2013)

Wimber, John, *Power Evangelism* (London: Hodder and Stoughton, 1985)

Winfrey, Rebecca, *The Cross and Shame* (Cambridge: Grove Books, 2019)

Woolmer, John, *The Devil Goes Missing* (Oxford: Lion Hudson, 2017)

Wright, N.T., *How God Became King: The Forgotten Story of the Gospels* (London: HarperCollins, 2012), Kindle edition

Wright, Tom, *The Day The Revolution Began: Rethinking the Meaning of Jesus' Crucifixion* (London: SPCK, 2016)

Zens, Jon, *58 to 0: How Christ Leads Through the One Anothers* (Omaha, NE: Ekklesia Press, 2013)

Zizioulas, John D., *Being as Communion* (London: Darton, Longman & Todd, 1985, 2004).

Zizioulas, John D., *Communion and Otherness* (Edinburgh: T&T Clark, 2006)